The GUINNESS Book of
Mammals

The GUINNESS Book of

MAMMALS

John A Burton

Line drawings by Jean Vaughan

GUINNESS SUPERLATIVES LIMITED
2 CECIL COURT, LONDON ROAD, ENFIELD, MIDDLESEX

29906

© Guideway Publishing Ltd 1982

Designed and produced by Guideway Publishing Ltd
Willow House, 27-49 Willow Way, London SE26

Published in 1982 by Guinness Superlatives Ltd,
2 Cecil Court, London Road, Enfield, Middlesex EN2 6DJ

Guinness is a registered trademark of
Guinness Superlatives Ltd

Burton, John A.
Mammals.—(Natural heritage)
1. Mammals
I. Title II. Series
599   QL703
ISBN 0-85112-305-8

O1a55 1

Printed and bound in Spain by Mateu Cromo Artes Gráficas, S.A. Pinto (Madrid)

Maps by David Perrott

The publishers wish to thank the following for their permission
to reproduce photographs: *Aquila Photographics:* 51 (Liz & Tony Bomford);
129 (J. Andrewartha). *Ardea London Ltd:* 69, 91, 115, 127, 131 (I. & L.
Beames); 71 (John Mason); 73 (Werner Curth); 83 (Abe Lindau); 107 (R. J. C.
Blewitt); 113 (Liz & Tony Bomford); 137 (R. & V. Taylor); 145 (C. K. Mylne).
Biofotos: 95, 101, 143 (Heather Angel); 121, 123 (Geoffrey Kinns). *Bruce
Coleman Ltd:* 57, 59, 65, 75 (Jane Burton); 61, 63, 67, 77, 79, 119 (S. C.
Bisserot); 85 (Kim Taylor); 89 (Eric Crichton); 99 (S. C. Porter);
103 (John Markham); 105 (P. A. Hinchliffe); 109, 117, 125 (Hans Reinhard);
133 (M. P. L. Fogden); 135, 139 (Ken Balcomb); 141 (G. Williamson); 147
(Udo Hirsch); 149 (Francisco Erize). *David Hosking:* 53, 55, 97. *Nature
Photographers Ltd:* 87, 111 (S. C. Bisserot); 93 (Owen Newman). *Oxford
Scientific Films Ltd:* 81 (Robert Maier).

Front Cover: Wild Cats

Contents

Introduction

From the emergence of the study of natural history in the late eighteenth and early nineteenth centuries until well into this century, most naturalists were concerned almost exclusively with the collection of specimens—skins, shells, pinned insects or pressed flowers—although bird*watching* was well established. However, over the last three or four decades, the growing tendency among naturalists, both amateur and professional, to observe all forms of wildlife rather than to collect them, has also led to an increased interest in the conservation and protection of wildlife, and it is difficult, even with hindsight, to say which came first— a public interest in wildlife or a concern for conservation.

Knowledge and information are important parts of conservation and this book is intended to provide a background of data about the mammals of the British Isles, with a definite slant towards their conservation. The need to protect these mammals will be self-evident after glancing at a few pages, such are the effects that man has had on the natural environment. Today, most of the wildlife of these islands, other than a handful of so-called pest species, are threatened in some way or another.

Surprisingly, since mammals are generally accredited with being among the more intelligent of animals—and, therefore, closer to man—protection for mammals has lagged far behind that for birds. At the turn of the century, organisations such as the Society for the Preservation of Fauna of the Empire (now the Fauna and Flora Preservation Society) were successfully lobbying for protective legislation on behalf of the larger mammals in Africa, but this was really only an extension of game law, and it is only in the last few decades that the conservation of mammals such as bats and rodents has become a serious issue. It is hoped that this book will place *all* the mammals of Britain and Ireland in a conservation perspective.

The History of Mammal Fauna

The history of the mammal fauna of the British Isles is closely connected with that of man. From earliest times some species have been important as food animals, some have competed with man's livestock, while others have preyed on his livestock and crops. In addition to the direct interactions between man and wild mammals, man has modified to a greater or lesser degree almost all habitats in the British Isles and this in turn has affected the mammalian fauna.

The first major events affecting the mammal fauna of the islands had nothing to do with man; these were the series of glaciations of the Pleistocene period, usually known as the Ice Ages. The last of these Ice Ages (the *Würm*) started some 20 000 years ago and finished about 10 000 years later. (In fact, it is quite possible that we are at present living in an interstadial—a warm period between Ice Ages—and that the ice could return any time.) As the ice cap retreated, which at its greatest extent reached as far south as Oxford, so the flora and fauna followed.

For hundreds of years after the last period of glaciation, as the climate ameliorated, Ireland was connected to Wales and England was joined to France and the Low Countries, the Thames joining with the Rhine to flow northwards through a land which is now the Dogger Bank in the North Sea. The mammals which had adapted to the rigours of a near arctic climate were the first to spread northwards, among them the stoat and the varying or mountain hare. Both of these were able to colonise Ireland, and in isolation the Irish hare has largely lost the ability to change its coat.

Only relatively few mammals had colonised Ireland by the time it was cut off from the rest of Britain at least 8000 years ago. Exactly which species had reached Ireland is difficult to ascertain, for man has introduced and translocated many species throughout history and prehistory, both deliberately and accidentally, but the pygmy shrew, hedgehog, pine marten, otter, fox, badger and red deer had probably got there of their own accord. The long-tailed mouse and red squirrel may have been introduced, and the rest of Ireland's mammal fauna (other than bats and marine species) are almost certainly a result of man's deliberate or unwitting help.

About 5000 years ago, England's connection with continental Europe was severed. Although many more species had crossed what is now the English Channel than had reached Ireland, a number of species which eventually spread to northern France and the Low Countries did not manage to reach the north before the sea inundated the Channel. These species included the greater white-toothed shrew (*Crocidura russula*) and bi-coloured white-toothed shrew (*C. leucodon*), garden dormouse (*Eliomys quercinus*), common vole (*Microtus arvalis*), pine vole (*Pitymys subterraneus*), beech marten (*Martes foina*), Nathusius' pipistrelle (*Pipistrellus nathusii*),

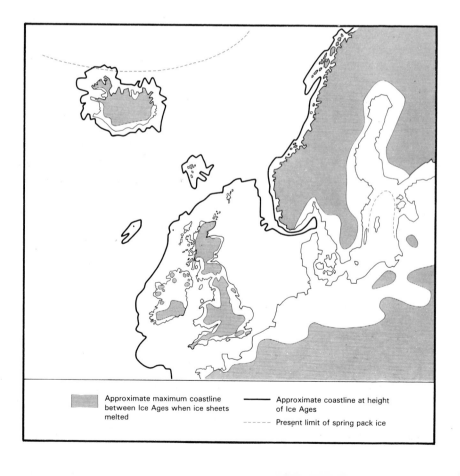

Approximate maximum coastline between Ice Ages when ice sheets melted	Approximate coastline at height of Ice Ages
	Present limit of spring pack ice

Geoffroy's bat (*Myotis emarginatus*) and pond bat (*Myotis dasyc-neme*); however, a single specimen of Nathusius' pipistrelle has since been recorded in Britain—showing that bats, being more mobile than the other species, are able to cross the Channel.

At the same time as some species were colonising, others were probably already being exterminated or disappearing from natural causes. Earlier, in the Pleistocene period, mammoths, woolly rhinoceroses, hyenas, lions and a whole range of large mammals had at various time roamed Britain, giving it an appearance akin to modern East Africa. Most of these animals subsequently disappeared from Britain and the rest of Europe. Within historic times, the list of lost animals is much smaller. The lynx, although often thought of as one of Britain's more recently extinct species, did not survive into the neolithic era. Nor did the reindeer: in palaeolithic sites reindeer remains abound, but the few remains of reindeer from Iron Age sites are in Scotland and can be attributed to imports by Norse traders; the one literary reference to reindeer, the Orkneyinga Saga, which records events of the middle of the twelfth century, can be dismissed as being written by someone who did not know the differences between red deer, roe deer and reindeer.

The brown bear was undoubtedly a member of the British fauna within historic times. For instance, imports of bears from Britain into Rome for use in beasthunts and shows in arenas such as the Colosseum are well documented, and in Wales place-names incorporating *arth* (she-bear) are found in remote areas. However, there is no evidence of bears surviving in Britain much after the eighth century.

The next animal to disappear was the beaver. The documentary evidence for the beaver's former occurrence is substantial, and place-names such as Beverley, Bewerley, Beverton and Beaverbrook are widespread. Giraldus Cambrensis, who travelled through Wales in 1188, left a full and detailed account of the beavers on the River Teifi. The cause of the beaver's extinction was probably a combination of hunting for its luxuriant fur and its musk glands, which were sought after by apothecaries; furthermore, beavers' tails, because of their fish-like appeareance, could be eaten during Lent. As a result of this predation by man, by the twelfth century, the beaver was probably extinct in Britain.

The mammal which vanished next was the wild boar. It is somewhat surprising that the boar became extinct since, as an animal of the chase, it was often protected, and elsewhere in Europe it has survived, even in quite densely populated areas. Throughout the medieval

12

Some mammals that were present in the British Isles during the Pleistocene period: (a) giant elk, (b) woolly mammoth, (c) woolly rhinoceros, (d) hyena (e) cave bear, and (f) cave lion.

period, boar were abundant throughout the forests which covered much of lowland Britain, but by the reign of Henry VIII they were becoming scarce in the south of England, and by 1600 they were very rare south of the Trent. During the Civil War the remaining stocks, mostly enclosed in parks, were further reduced and the last one was recorded in 1676 in Cannock Chase in Staffordshire. The New Forest was stocked with imported boar until the end of the eighteenth century, when they too disappeared. In Ireland the boar was described by Giraldus Cambrensis as being very abundant, but they, too, became extinct sometime in the seventeenth century.

The last large native British mammal to become extinct was the wolf. Like the beaver the widespread occurrence of the wolf is recorded in numerous place-names such as Wolfpit, Woodale, Louvenbowe, Howl Moor, Wolvescote Dale. But throughout its history in Britain, the wolf was ruthlessly persecuted and there usually was a bounty on it. By Elizabethan times the wolf was already a rare animal, confined to the more remote moors and mountainous areas and probably extinct in England. The last wolf killed in Wales was in the late eighteenth century, in Ireland around 1770, and in Scotland in 1743.

Before concluding these comments on Britain's extinct fauna, mention should be made of the marine species. The walrus occurred on the coasts of Britain within historic times, and it is possible that it may have even bred around the northern islands. The 18-m (60 ft) Atlantic or Biscayan right whale (so called because it was the 'right' species to kill) was once found in British waters, and was the basis of a whaling industry in the Bay of Biscay. At this time, much of France was under British rule, and so Edward II's edict of 1324 making whales 'Fishes Royal' takes on considerably more significance when it is realised that the Crown thereby owned the rights to a highly profitable industry. This industry was the direct ancestor of modern factory-ship whaling, which has reduced most of the great whales to the brink of extinction. The decline of the right whales in coastal European waters led to the Basque whalers going further and further afield, eventually, in 1611 under British captaincy, as far as Spitzbergen in the Arctic. By the middle of the nineteenth century the Atlantic right whale was thought to be extinct; however, a few were killed in the 1890s off Iceland and then some 67 were killed in Scottish waters from 1908 to 1914. Even a take of such small numbers probably had a disastrous effect on the remnant population of the Atlantic right whale, and even now its continued existence is uncertain.

While these mammals were disappearing, others were arriving, often with the aid of man. Rats, mice, grey squirrel, rabbit, coypu, mink, several species of deer and one of dormouse have all arrived in the British Isles with man's help. Most of the offshore islands, particularly the more northerly, were populated with rats, mice and voles which travelled with man, and the Isles of Scilly are now populated with the lesser white-toothed shrew (*Crocidura suaveolens*), which probably came with man from Iberia. On some of the Scottish islands the mice, in particular, have evolved into animals markedly different from their mainland neighbours, with a numbers of subspecies now being recognised. In Ireland, in addition to some of the species mentioned above, the bank vole also occurs as a result of an introduction which probably took place in the early 1960s.

Some of Britain's mammals remained unnoticed until comparatively recently. For example, the parson-naturalist of Selborne, Gilbert White, was the first to draw attention to the harvest mouse in 1767. From his letters to Thomas Pennant and Daines Barrington (which were first published in 1788), it can be concluded that he had first-hand experience of at least 21 mammals around the Selborne area on the Surrey/Hampshire border. Several of these have now disappeared from there or are much rarer—for instance, the polecat, otter, red squirrel and dormouse. However, White only recognised three species of bats, and did not record roe deer, voles, water shrews and several other species which were probably to be found in his neighbourhood.

The yellow-necked mouse was first described from Britain as recently as 1894, but it is among the bats that the most recent discoveries have been made. The mouse-eared bat, which may now be extinct, was first described in 1956 (although there are isolated records from 1888 and before); the grey long-eared bat was not noticed until 1964, although on close examination of museum specimens it was shown that it has probably always been present in small numbers. Similarly, on close examination of whiskered bats, it was recently shown that another species, Brandt's bat (*Myotis brandti*) also occurs and is, in fact, widespread and quite abundant. Although only a single specimen has been recorded so far, Nathusius' pipistrelle has also been discovered recently and may be present in small numbers.

The recording of marine mammals is much more difficult and it is only in the last decade or so that any organised attempts have been made to document sightings. Since early this century, detailed records of strandings have been kept and now approximately 25 species of whales, dolphins, and porpoises have been recorded from the waters around the British Isles. Improved field identification techniques, together with a greater interest and more sophisticated optical and photographic equipment, are leading to an increasing number of reliable sight records of cetaceans.

The Names of Mammals

Because of their long and close association with man, names have been given to mammals which reflect the various derivations of the English language. The best examples are of domestic and game animals. Live domestic animals, and their wild ancestors, tended to be given names derived from Anglo-Saxon, but were given names derived from old French when these animals were ready for the table. For example, the animal is called 'ox' or 'calf' alive, but 'beef' or 'veal' when dead, the same being true for 'sheep' and 'mutton', 'deer' and 'venison', 'pig' or 'boar' and 'pork'. This duality very pointedly demonstrates the fact that, while Anglo-Saxon peasants tended the animals, it was their Norman conquerors who actually ate them! Similarly, the very elaborate vocabulary of the chase, which became highly developed in the Middle Ages, is almost entirely based on the language of the Norman French court.

From the eighteenth century, the names of animals came to play an increasingly important part in the advancement of scientific knowledge. The Swedish naturalist, Carl von Linné, usually known as Linnaeus, is often accredited with being the first person to classify animals using the binomial, or 'two-name', system. In fact, others had done this before him, but Linnaeus did it on a more comprehensive and organised scale than anyone else. It was his system that was to provide the entire basis for naming all animals and plants that is still in use throughout the world; even scientific works in languages such as Chinese and Russian incorporate these Latin names. The two names —the genus and the species—are in a form of Latin which is often very much distorted. The first is the generic name (which begins with a capital letter), followed by the specific name, the latter relating to the particular type of animal, while the genus groups similar species together. Above the species and genus are other groupings such as 'family', 'order' and 'class' which are, in turn, further grouped and subdivided (according to the whims of the scientists studying the classification of animals—taxonomists and systematists) into sub-families, super-species, etc.

At the time when Linnaeus developed his Latin-based names for animals and plants, Latin was the scientific lingua-franca and, until comparatively recent times, held this position for the description of new species. Although animals are no longer usually written about in Latin, the names still remain a common language among scientists and naturalists, and in many cases the vernacular names are little better than transliterations or translations of the Latin names. Obviously, the universal use of Latin does much to avoid language problems. *Myotis brandti* is a species which mammalogists throughout Europe will recognise; but the English name—Brandt's whiskered bat—might cause confusion. The name 'common vole' might be one of several species depending on where you are, but all biologists would know what is meant by *Microtus agrestis* or *Microtus arvalis* (in English, 'field vole' and 'common vole' respectively).

Although many of these names are based on the names of the mammals in Latin or Latinised Greek—such as *Cervus* (deer) or *Phoca* (seals)—almost as many are based on the names of scientists (e.g., *daubentoni*), the attributes of the animals (*vulgaris* = common) or occurrence (*nippon* = Japan). In addition, while knowing the meanings of the Latin names may in some cases act as an *aide-mémoire*, it is worth remembering that they can also be misleading since opinions as to their attributes may well have changed since the animals were first described.

Species and Subspecies

When the *List of British Mammals* (which includes the Channel Islands) was published by the British Museum (Natural History) in 1964, there were 95 species of mammals found in Britain. Of these, 23 were cetaceans—whales, dolphins, porpoises, etc.—seven were species of seals and 15 of bats. Seven species had become extinct within historic times; three were listed as feral and 19 were introduced —in fact, 38 per cent of our terrestrial mammals have been introduced into the British Isles at some point in their history. Since this list was first prepared (by Dr G. B. Corbet), the overall picture has remained much the same. In this book, native species and the more established introductions are dealt with in the chapter on specific species.

Large numbers of species and subspecies were described in the late nineteenth and early twentieth century, but when the majority of these were examined closely, and a large sample of animals checked, the differences rarely appeared as well marked as the earlier naturalists had thought. However, in isolation, new species do tend to evolve, and subspecies are best considered as species in the process of evolution. In general, habitats such as those on islands, particularly small islands, tend to accentuate the differences between populations.

In the British Museum (Natural History) list, three subspecies of common shrew are recognised: *Sorex araneus castaneus* on mainland Britain, *S.a. fretalis* on Jersey and *S.a. granti* on the island of Islay in the Hebrides. The British water shrew is distinguished from continental populations by the name *Neomys fodiens bicolor*, which refers to its normal black and white pelage. The white-toothed shrew of the Isles of Scilly, although probably introduced by man, is sufficiently different as to be considered a separate subspecies: *Crocidura suaveolens cassiteridum*.

There are three subspecies which are recognised for both the stoat and the polecat. The stoat is seen as the Irish stoat (*Mustela erminea hibernica*), the race of Britain proper (*M.e. stabilis*) and the race inhabiting Islay and Jura in the Hebrides, *M.e. ricinae*. Of the polecats, the domesticated ferret (*Mustela putorius furo*) and the Welsh polecat (*M.p. anglia*) are both expanding their ranges; on the other hand, the Scottish polecat (*M.p. caledoniae*), not recognised until

1939, had become extinct around 1912.

Of the larger mammals, the Scottish wild cat (*Felis silvestris grampia*) is one of Britain's more distinctive animals, being generally larger than those of southern Europe. However, the red deer of Britain (*Cervus elaphus scoticus*) are dubiously distinct from continental animals—those of Scotland are small, but this is largely due to their poor diet.

The brown hare has been described as a separate race (*Lepus capensis occidentalis*), and the Scottish and Irish populations of the varying hare are considered separate subspecies (respectively, *Lepus timidus scoticus* and *L.t. hibernicus*). Indeed, the latter, which does not change colour, has often been regarded as a distinct species. The British red squirrel (*Sciurus vulgaris leucourus*) is also one of the more distinctive races, but introductions from the Continent, in particular those from Germany, have caused some confusion.

The differentiation of species in isolation on islands is best seen in some of the small mammals. Large numbers of subspecies have been described for mice and voles, many of which are quite distinctive. There are 15 races of wood mice to be found on Scottish and Irish islands, many of which are very much larger than the mainland populations: *Apodemus sylvaticus hebridensis* on the Outer Hebrides; *A.s. hirtensis* on St Kilda; *A.s. fridariensis* on Fair Isle; *A.s. butie* on Bute; *A.s. cumbrae* on Great Cumbrae Island; *A.s. maclean* on Mull; *A.s. hamiltoni* on Rum (Rhum); *A.s. fiologan* on Arran; *A.s. granti* on Shetland; *A.s. thuleo* on Foula; *A.s. tirae* on Tiree; *A.s. tural* on Islay; *A.s. ghia* on Gigha; *A.s. larus* on Jura; and *A.s. nesiticus* on Mingulay. Many of these mice are so large that, at one time, they were thought to be related to the yellow-necked mouse, the British population of which is separated as *Apodemus flavicollis wintoni*. One

A wood mouse and (left) a Hebridean wood mouse *(Apodemus sylvaticus hebridensis)*: many subspecies which have developed in isolation are much larger than the more common species.

famous island subspecies was the very distinctive house mouse of the island of St Kilda, *Mus musculus muralis*, which became extinct about 1932, soon after the human population was evacuated from the island. Like the wood mice, the field voles have evolved into many island subspecies: on Eigg, *Microtus agrestis mial* occurs; on Muck, *M.a. luch*; on Islay, *M.a. macgillivrayi*; and on Gigha, *M.a. fiona*. The closely related common vole of Orkney, *Microtus arvalis*, was probably introduced and has evolved into separate subspecies on most islands: *M.a. orcadensis* on Mainland (Orkney); *M.a. sandayensis* on Sanday and Westray; *M.a. ronaldshaiensis* on South Ronaldsay; *M.a. rousaiensis* on Rousay; and another subspecies *M.a. sarnius*, occurs on Guernsey in the Channel Islands.

Among the bank voles, distinctive subspecies have been found on Mull (*Clethrionomys glareolus alstoni*); on Skomer Island (*C.g. skomerensis*); on Raasay (*C.g. erica*) and Jersey (*C.g. caesarius*). It should not be forgotten, however, that Great Britain as a whole is an *island* country, and many animals, including those already mentioned, have developed unique characteristics in isolation from the Continent. Another example of this is the occurrence of two races of water vole, *Arvicola terrestris terrestris* in England, Wales and lowland Scotland, and *A.t. reta* in the Scottish Highlands.

Introductions and Feral Mammals

A previous chapter described how the colonisation of the British Isles by mammals took place over many thousands of years. However, this colonisation still continues via introductions which may or may not survive into the future. In addition, some of man's domestic animals have reverted to a wild state, and these feral animals further add to the diversity of the mammal population of the British Isles.

Introductions

Perhaps the most spectacular introduced mammal in Britain is the red-necked (Bennett's) wallaby (*Macropus rufogriseus*) from Australia, which grows to about 100 cm (39 in) with a further 75 cm (30 in) of tail; in general shape it is very like a kangaroo. Two small colonies—one in the Peak District and the other in Sussex—have existed since the early 1940s, though the captive stock from which they are descended had been present for much longer.

Large animals are not the only species to be introduced. In addition to the red-toothed (pygmy and common) shrews and water shrews, both of which are present in the British Isles, in most areas of continental Europe there is also usually at least one species of white-toothed shrew (*Crocidura* spp.). However, within the British Isles it is only in the Isles of Scilly and Channel Islands that any of these latter species occur. Similarly, a close relative of the field vole (*Microtus agrestis*) which is common in Britain, the common vole (*M. arvalis*) is widespread and abundant on the other side of the Channel, but only found in the Channel Islands and Orkney. Both the white-toothed shrews and common voles were probably introduced—albeit unwittingly—by man. It is likely that the Orkney voles (together with wood mice) came on Viking ships from Scandinavia, and the shrews to the Channel Isles from France and to the Scilles from Iberia. At one time hamsters managed to become established in the wild, but were later exterminated; however, more recently the Mongolian gerbil (*Meriones unguiculatus*) has become established in the Isle of Wight. By 1976 the colony there numbered over 100 and is potentially a serious pest, since in Asia and Africa gerbils do enormous amounts of damage to crops.

The threat posed by certain species of pests is well exemplified by porcupines which, in their native habitat, often do serious damage to root and other crops. Two species have escaped in England: the Hodgson's porcupine (*Hystrix hodgsoni*) and the crested porcupine (*H. cristata*). The former is a native of the central and eastern Himalayas eastwards to China and Malaysia; the crested porcupine occurs in Africa and also (probably as a result of introductions) in Italy and Yugoslavia. Himalayan porcupines escaped from Pine Valley Wildlife Park in Devon in 1969, and by 1973 were doing considerable damage to forestry plantations. In 1972 a pair of crested porcupines escaped from Alton Towers Botanic Garden, Staffordshire. Whether or not either species will survive for long remains to be seen, but if they do, they will probably continue to cause extensive damage to forestry and agriculture.

Domestic Animals and their Feral Relations

In a number of parts of Britain there are wild or semi-wild populations of man's domestic animals, the most impressive being the white park cattle and feral goats. In shape, if not in colour, the cattle resemble the aurochs, an extinct European wild ox. They have been preserved in parks such as Chillingham (Northumberland), Chartley (Staffordshire), Cadzow (Strathclyde) and Dynevor (Dyfed), and more recently in zoos such as Whipsnade (Bedfordshire). It has been speculated that they derive from ancient sacred cattle which were taken over by monasteries with the conversion of Britain to Christianity; after the Dissolution under Henry VIII the monasteries and their cattle fell into private hands. Even as recently as the end of the last century, the then Prince of Wales stalked and shot one of these 'wild' cattle—although, in those days, the bulls were often very aggressive.

The wild goats of the British Isles are shaggy-coated, long-horned animals, and apparently have a long history. Until comparatively recently, goats were kept on a very wide scale; in fact, until the eighteenth century and the agricultural revolution, goats and sheep were the mainstay of much of the dairying in Britain, oxen and cows being mainly meat and draught animals. This fact is often confused since, in early accounts, the word 'cattle' also included sheep and goats. There can be no doubt that the wild goats living in the British Isles were constantly intermixed with domestic breeds. The surviving herds, and there are a surprising number of them, are fairly widely distributed.

On some Scottish and Welsh islands there are sheep which are virtually wild. The most famous are the Soay sheep, principally found on the island of Hirta in St Kilda but they have also been introduced to Ailsa Craig, Cardigan Island and Lundy; in Orkney, seaweed-eating sheep survive.

On the moors and mountains of some of the wilder parts of the British Isles, ponies have survived in a semi-wild state, although intermixture with domestic stock has always taken place. There are a large number of place-names referring to horses, which were clearly places where they roamed free, such as Stodmarsh and Studland ('stud' derives from the Old English for 'mare'), and up to 100 years ago horses, wild and semi-wild, roamed many of the marshes, moors,

A feral goat.

heaths and mountains. The remaining 'wild' ponies are now found on Bodmin Moor, Exmoor, Dartmoor, in the New Forest and other places. The New Forest ponies are probably the most famous, but are now little more than a domesticated breed allowed free range for most of the year, having been 'improved', in the nineteenth century by Prince Albert, by the addition of Arab blood, and by much other interbreeding in that century. The Exmoor pony is probably the most primitive of the British native breeds, and closest to its ancestor, the tarpan, which died out in the Ukraine in the 1880s. Now these ponies and the Connemarra of Ireland, the Welsh mountain ponies and others are all very much domesticated strains.

In many parts of the British Isles feral cats live almost totally independently of man (dogs rarely survive in the feral state for more than one generation). In addition, ferrets, a domesticated form of the polecat used by rabbiters, frequently escape and survive in the wild. They were also deliberately introduced in Mull in the Hebrides in the 1930s and probably still survive, the polecat population there almost certainly containing an admixture of ferret.

The Future

It is of course impossible to accurately predict which mammals are likely to join Britain's fauna. But among the species which are possible are South American rodents—chinchillas and cavies—which are commonly bred in captivity; their native habitats include ones similar to some found in Britain. Another rodent from South America, the capybara, has escaped, and could survive in East Anglia.

There are several species of deer which breed prolifically in captivity and, should they escape, could easily become established; these include the white-tailed deer and the axis (spotted deer). Many small rodents, including a wide variety of chipmunks, rats, mice, hamsters and agoutis, could become established if they were introduced into a suitable area. Californian sea lions, released by zoos and circuses, have survived in the Mediterranean, and presumably they could also survive and even breed around Britain. In most cases, introductions would be relatively easy to exterminate should the animals prove a pest—but as the coypu, mink and grey squirrel have all shown, it is not always possible.

Finally, the question must be asked—what is a pest? To a farmer, a coypu is a pest, but to a naturalist it is surely an asset—particularly when it undermines neat river banks. Left to the coypu, the dikes and canals of East Anglia would gradually revert to their previous state as meandering swamps. Another supposed pest, the mink, is only filling a niche left vacant by the disappearance of native predators such as the pine marten, polecat and otter. Even the grey squirrel may be merely filling a niche from which the native red squirrel would have disappeared anyway (*see* page 86).

To a naturalist, probably the only true 'pest' is a species which brings another to extinction. Few, if any, of the species introduced into Britain have done this.

Identification

With most wild mammals in Britain, the main problem in identification is getting a good view of them, or being able to examine them closely enough to see the necessary details. The larger mammals such as deer and the carnivores are generally shy and elusive, and often nocturnal, while the smaller mammals such as shrews, bats, mice and other rodents often need to be examined in the hand to be identified positively. Whales and dolphins, unless stranded, are usually observed in fleeting glimpses as they come to the surface, and mammals such as moles or hedgehogs are rarely seen alive, although they are not infrequently found dead. However, the tracks and signs that

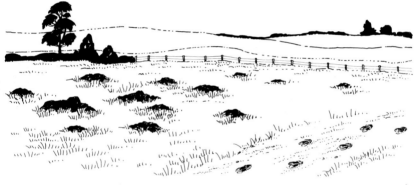

Mole-hills (tumps) and deer tracks (slots).

mammals leave are often very distinctive — ranging from the well-known 'tumps' (mole-hills) of moles to the neatly gnawed hazelnuts of mice, the footprints ('slots') of deer and the 'spraints' of otters.

Unlike birds, it is difficult to generalise when giving guidance on identification techniques for mammals. Instead it is necessary to treat each group of mammals separately.

Bats

Bats are extremely difficult to identify with certainty, even in the hand. It should be borne in mind, however, that bats are sensitive to disturbance and some species are protected and should not be handled. The important features to look for at close range are size, the shape of the ear and tragus (lobe on the edge of the ear), and fur colour. In flight, note the size, speed and type of flight (fluttering, swooping, etc.). By using ultrasonic receivers, it is possible to identify some bats by their calls.

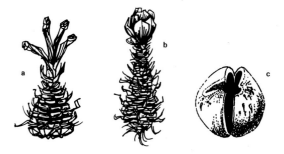

Food remains of squirrels: (a) stripped pine cone and (b) spruce cone; (c) gnawed hazelnut.

Shrews, Voles, Rats and Mice

Superficially mice, shrews and voles are very similar; however, voles have rather blunt heads and proportionally shorter tails than mice, shrews have very pointed snouts, very small eyes and velvety fur, and mice have rather long tails and large eyes. Shrews can often be heard squeaking in hedgerows; they are rarely seen, although sometimes they are found dead, for no apparent reason, lying on paths. The jaws

Bank vole's store of nuts and berries.

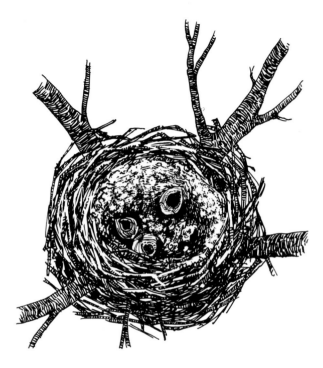

Old birds' nest used as feeding platform by wood mice or yellow-necked mice.

and teeth of all species can be easily identified when found in owl pellets or empty bottles (*see* page 33). With the aid of a key (a good one is found in Lawrence and Brown's book, *see* page 38), it is fairly easy to identify most British species fairly quickly.

The food remains of mice are often characteristic. Rats and mice leave a distinctive odour when they spoil food stores as well as leaving easily identifiable droppings and general damage. Wood and yellow-necked mice often use old birds' nests as feeding platforms and accumulations of the remains of haws, hips and other berries and nuts are characteristic. The nests of harvest mice are best searched for in winter when vegetation has died back.

Carnivores

Badgers and foxes are occasionally seen, even in daylight, but their setts and earths (respectively) are distinctive; fresh footprints, pathways, tufts of hair attached to barbed wire and many other signs also indicate their presence. Weasels, stoats, mink and polecats are elusive, but occasionally glimpsed. The otter is rarely seen, but often leaves characteristically smelling 'spraints' on rocky promontories.

Hares and Rabbits
Hares are larger and longer legged than rabbits, and often in more open country. The black tips to the hares' ears are distinctive.

Deer
Deer are easily seen in certain situations, such as parks, but more often they are shy and elusive. They leave identifiable tracks ('slots') and signs, such as fraying (abrading bushes and trees) and droppings. Features to look for in the live animal are size, shape of antlers, rump pattern and general colouring.

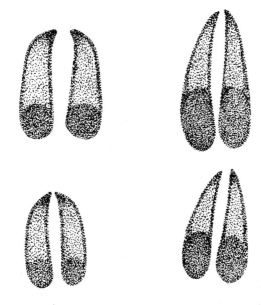

Deer 'slots' (tracks): red deer (left) and fallow deer.

Seals
Very often only the head of a seal is seen above water, and its shape and size are important in identification. Although common and grey

seals are normally the only species found around the British Isles, others have been recorded.

Whales, Dolphins and Porpoises

Unless found stranded on a beach, when measurements and photographs can be taken and teeth examined, most whales and dolphins are glimpsed momentarily as they come to the surface to breathe. In the case of the larger whales, the shape, height and direction of the 'blow' are often diagnostic. With all whales, the size, shape and position of the dorsal fin are important identification aids. Other features to look for include pattern behaviour, such as pitchpoling, breaching and bow wave riding.

Studying Mammals

Relatively few naturalists go mammal-watching in the same way as other people go birdwatching, botanising, rock-pooling or butterfly-catching. The reason for this is quite simple: most mammals are rarely seen. Even large, theoretically easily observed species, such as deer, hares and rabbits, are often extremely shy and mainly active at night. To study mammals a variety of indirect methods are used, and direct observation may need technological aids as well as patience.

Direct observation
Most of the larger mammals can, on occasion, be observed in the field, and the basic equipment needed is similar to that used by bird-watchers. Binoculars are often used at twilight or in moonlight, so those with good light-gathering powers, such as 7 × 50s or even 8 × 30s, can be useful. A good pair of binoculars and a lot of patience are all that are needed for watching species such as badgers, foxes, deer and rabbits. Even these can be dispensed with in some places—for instance, where squirrels are so tame as to feed from the hand, and where foxes have become completely accustomed to man.

For whale-watching, good, powerful binoculars are needed and, if watching from land, a telescope and tripod are an advantage.

In addition, infra-red viewing equipment, redlights, light intensi-fiers and radio tracking have all become part of the equipment used by scientists studying nocturnal mammals.

Trapping
Various live traps are available, the best known being the Longworth; by setting a series of traps at regular intervals on successive nights, a good idea of the small mammal fauna in a given area can be gained. Natural history societies, schools and colleges often keep traps for this purpose. Pitfall traps (large jars sunk in runs) are also effective. All traps should be checked every few hours since shrews die of starvation very quickly.

Birds-of-prey pellets
Most birds of prey (eagles, hawks, falcons and owls) regurgitate

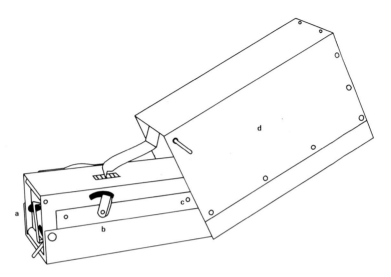

A Longworth live trap. The animal goes through the entrance (a), then travels through the tunnel (b). At its end (c), there is a treadle which the animal depresses. This releases a door which swings down and locks behind the animal as it enters the nesting box (d).

pellets composed of the teeth, bones and other indigestible parts of their prey. Since these pellets are often produced at the bird's regular roosting site, by gathering the pellets and dissecting them, it is possible to identify the small mammals from the surrounding countryside which form the bird's prey. These remnants, particularly teeth, skulls and jaws, are fairly easy to identify with the aid of a key; a good one is to be found in the book by Lawrence and Brown (*see* page 38).

Discarded bottles
The general public are extremely untidy and the countryside, unhappily, generally abounds in litter, among which there are usually numerous bottles. Unfortunately, small mammals are usually very inquisitive and will often climb inside bottles to investigate them; once inside, the slope of the neck, combined with wetness from any rainwater or other liquid dampening their fur and sticking to the glass, often prevent the animal from climbing out. When it has died, the insects attracted by the corpse in turn attract shrews and other species to their doom. Over 20 animals in varying stages of decomposition can sometimes be found in a single bottle; practically all small mammals up to the size of a weasel can be found. Usually, the contents of the

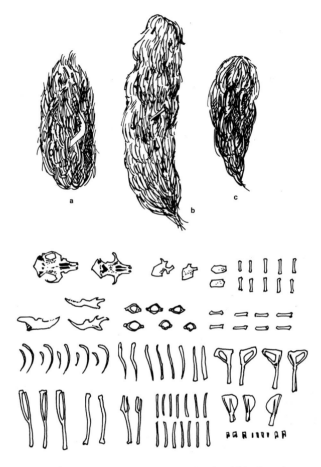

Bird-of-prey pellets from (a) a tawny owl, (b) a short-eared owl and (c) a kestrel, with (below) the variety of prey remains to be found when these are dissected.

bottle are in the form of a putrifying and foul-smelling black liquid with bones and rotting flesh floating in it, although in some cases freshly dead corpses can be found. The technique for identifying the remains is similar to that used for birds-of-prey pellets.

Studying bats

The techniques for studying bats are rather different from other species. If studying them at their roosts, it is important to remember that they are extremely sensitive to disturbance and that licences are needed to handle certain protected species. For counting bats leaving roosts, hand tally counters are useful, as are binoculars. Electronic 'bat detectors' have been developed which make audible the high-frequency sound emissions of bats' sonar; the human ear does not register much above 20 Hz whereas the sounds emitted by a bat can reach 120 Hz. The resultant pulses are often characteristic and certain species can be identified with confidence in this way. Tape recordings made on sophisticated machines sensitive to the range of sounds used by bats can also be used; tapes are then slowed down to produce sounds audible to humans.

Photography

Photographing wild mammals is usually extremely difficult except for a few species in certain situations, for example, seals at their breeding rookeries, squirrels in city parks and deer in parks. For other wild mammals, fairly sophisticated equipment with a range of lenses, flashes and even automatic releases may be needed. Most small mammals are usually photographed under 'controlled' conditions, i.e., they are trapped and photographed in an enclosure or vivarium.

Notebooks and record-keeping

Like birdwatching and all other forms of natural history, a notebook is an important—if not essential—piece of equipment. There is still a remarkable amount to be learned about the basic behaviour of many of the mammals present in the British Isles and, by noting down all observations, new data can easily be accumulated—even by a beginner.

Even though the general distribution is known for most species, there are still many gaps, and in most parts of the country the detailed distribution has yet to be worked out for most species. Observations should always be accompanied by six-figure grid references taken from the 1:50 000 Ordnance Survey maps (or larger scale). The Biological Records Centre at the Institute of Terrestrial Ecology, Monk's Wood, Abbots Ripton, Cambridgeshire is the central collecting body for all biological records, but many local natural history societies also collect and publish records of mammals.

Monitoring Population Changes

The most obvious use of field observations of mammals, however scant, is for establishing their distribution. With this basic knowledge, it is then possible to develop more detailed studies of behaviour and to monitor population changes.

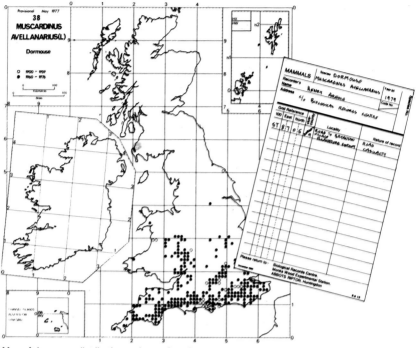

Map of dormouse distribution and record card
from the Biological Records Centre.

Mammal (and other animal) populations change in two ways—as entire species, or locally and within individual populations. For some species, it is possible to make total counts of at least part of the population, and it is then possible to monitor changes fairly accurately. This has, in fact, been done with seals which breed in the British Isles, and with deer in certain localities such as those on the island of Rum (Rhum). In addition to making counts, plotting an animal's distribution and noting changes also give an indication of changes in populations—a species which is spreading its range is invariably increasing in numbers, and vice versa. The distribution of a number of species has been studied in detail, in some cases over a considerable period of time; these include the grey and the red squirrel, dormouse, harvest mouse, badger, mink, otter, greater horseshoe bat, grey seal, coypu, rabbit, black rat and fox. Several of these are species of economic importance (such as the rabbit and coypu) and their populations are studied and monitored in some detail by the Ministry of Agriculture, Fisheries and Food.

Total counts of a species are, however, rarely possible. Some species, notably badgers, can be estimated by counting their setts; for example, it has been estimated that there are 1.8 setts per 1000 acres (2471 hectares) in Dorset and 0.1 setts per 1000 acres in Norfolk.

Sett

A badger's sett.

For most mammals, estimates have to be based on samples. This can either take the form of making a total count in a small area and multiplying up for the whole area known to be occupied, or by using mark recapture data. In the latter, animals are marked by a variety of methods including ringing, freeze branding, tagging, fur clipping and dyeing; the number of times they are recaptured gives a proportion of marked to unmarked animals in a population, and hence an estimate for the total. Proportions of species present in birds-of-prey pellets and those dying in discarded bottles (*see* page 33), although subject to other selective pressures, will also, over a period of time, give an indication of changes in abundance. By recording road casualties among species such as hedgehogs, population data can also be accumulated. Changes in hare populations have been noted in the records of shoots—and it appears that brown hares have declined greatly. Changes in bat populations—and bats as a group have declined disastrously in recent years—have been monitored by a combination of total counts, mark recapture and also by checking the existence of roosts recorded by the public over a period of several years.

With all the above methods there are a large number of factors which have to be taken into account when interpreting the results—for instance, when grid-trapping for samples of mammals, certain species are 'trap-shy' while others become trap addicts—and the expertise of the observer will influence all results.

Further Reading

This book is not intended to be a field guide for the identification of the species of mammals found in the British Isles. There are a number of books which perform this function, and there are also many books which will add to your knowledge about mammalian fauna in general and about specific types of mammals.

For beginners

J. Burton, *The Gem Guide to Wild Animals* (Collins, 1980); D. Ovenden, G. B. Corbet and E. N. Arnold, *Collins Handguide to the Wild Animals of Europe* (Collins, 1979).

Field identification guides

M. Burton, *Guide to the Mammals of Britain and Europe* (Elsevier/ Phaidon, 1976); G. B. Corbet and D. Ovenden, *The Mammals of Britain* (Collins, 1980); F. J. Taylor Page, *Field Guide to British Deer* (Blackwells, 1971).

Reference books

H. R. Arnold, *Provisional Atlas of the Mammals of the British Isles* (Natural Environment Research Council, 1978); R. Burton, *Carnivores of Europe* (Batsford, 1979); G. B. Corbet, *The Identification of British Mammals* (British Museum [Natural History], 1978); G. B. Corbet, *The Mammals of the Palearctic Region: A Taxonomic*

Review (Foulis, 1966); G. B. Corbet and H. N. Southern (eds.), *The Handbook of British Mammals* (Blackwell, 1977); P. G. H. Evans, 'Cetaceans in British Waters', *Mammal Review* (Vol. 10, No. 1, 1980); J. S. Fairley, *An Irish Beast Book* (Blackstaff, 1975); L. B. Halstead, *The Evolution of the Mammals* (Peter Lowe, 1978); H. R. Hewer, *British Seals* (Collins, 1974); B. Kurtén, *The Ice Age* (Rupert Hart-Davis, 1972); E. N. Lamhna (ed.), *Provisional Distribution Atlas of Amphibians, Reptiles and Mammals in Ireland* (An Foras Forbartha, 1979); M. J. Lawrence and R. W. Brown, *Mammals of Britain: Their Tracks, Trails and Signs* (Blandford, 2nd rev. ed. 1974); Leatherwood, Caldwell and Winn, *Whales, Dolphins and Porpoises of the Western Atlantic: A Guide to Their Identification* (National Oceanic and Atmospheric Administration [USA], 1976).

Conservation

The protection of mammals, for purposes other than hunting, is a very recent phenomenon in the British Isles. It is difficult to summarise and explain the laws relating to British mammals, since there is little or no apparent logic behind them. A mixture of game laws (deriving from ancient forest laws) and modern conservation laws, together with vermin controls and animal welfare legislation, produces an approach for which it is difficult to find a rationale.

The law that defines whales as 'Fishes Royal' dates back to medieval times. Deer are game with complicated legislation controlling how they may be killed. They are subject to the Deer Act (Scotland), 1959, and the Deer Act, 1963, both of which, although mainly concerned with the welfare of deer as game, also embody some conservation principles. Rabbits and hares are sometimes game, but at other times are vermin. Seals and badgers are both protected under special legislation—seals under the Conservation of Seals Act, 1970, which is usually considered the first conservation legislation, and badgers under the Badgers Act, 1973, which protects it everywhere except in areas where it can be implicated in the spread of bovine tuberculosis. However, despite the fact that pine martens, wild cats and polecats all have much more restricted ranges than badgers, the three aforementioned species are still unprotected in the United Kingdom.

This lack of a rational approach is not present in bird protection legislation which acts on the premise that most species of birds should be protected. It categorises birds into three groups: some rare species should be protected by the levying of special penalties; some should have protection reduced if a landowner can show damage was being caused; and, finally, a tiny minority should be unprotected as pest species. Unfortunately, this approach has yet to be adopted for animals other than birds.

In 1975 the Conservation of Wild Creatures and Wild Plants Act was passed in Great Britain, which gave protection to the greater horseshoe bat and the mouse-eared bat, and provided limited protection for other bats. Subsequently, the otter was given protection in England and Wales. At the time of writing the Wildlife and Coun-

A checklist of conservation legislation in the British Isles

● = protected
✱ = strictly protected
★ = does not occur

+ = protected but may be hunted at certain times of the year or in certain areas.

	Protected in the UK	Protected in Eire
Hedgehog		●
Common shrew		★
Pygmy shrew		●
Water shrew		★
Lesser white-toothed shrew		★
Mole		★
Whiskered bat	●	●
Natterer's bat	●	●
Daubenton's bat	●	
Long-eared bat	●	●
Grey long-eared bat	●	★
Bechstein's bat	●	★
Barbastelle	●	★
Pipistrelle	●	●
Noctule	●	★
Lesser noctule	●	●
Serotine	●	★
Greater horseshoe bat	✱	★
Lesser horseshoe bat	●	●
Mouse-eared bat	✱	★
Brown hare	+	●
Varying hare	+	●
Rabbit		
Grey Squirrel		
Red Squirrel		●

	Protected in the UK	Protected in Eire
Bank vole		
Field vole		★
Water vole		★
Common vole		★
Black rat		
Brown rat		
House mouse		
Harvest mouse		★
Wood mouse		
Yellow-necked mouse		★
Dormouse		★
Red fox		
Weasel		★
Stoat		●
Polecat		★
Pine marten		●
Otter	*	●
Badger	*	●
Wild cat		★
Fallow deer	+	
Red deer	+	
Roe deer	+	★
Common seal	+	●
Grey seal	+	●
Whales, dolphins, porpoises	*	●

tryside Bill is proceeding through Parliament which, if passed, would give protection to the otter in Scotland, extend the protection given to bats and possibly protect the red squirrel in England. With the more recent legislation, an attempt is being made to rationalise the legal status of wild animals. However, the powerful and influential 'huntin', shootin' and fishin'' lobby in Britain, together with farming interests, largely represented by the National Farmers' Union and the Ministry of Agriculture, Fisheries and Food, have ensured that the protection afforded to Britain's mammals remains minimal. As a consequence, certain methods of killing are prohibited (on the grounds that they are inhumane) for certain species but not for others. It would appear that it is permissible to be cruel to rats, mink, moles, grey squirrels and other vermin, but not to dormice or water shrews, even though these latter are not protected species.

Britain has often been regarded as one of the world's leaders in animal conservation and protection. In the past, this was undoubtedly true but it is not so now. The legal protection given to British reptiles, amphibians and mammals falls far short of most European countries, and even that of many developing countries. This is not to say that such legislation is always enforced—often it is not—but at least the intention is there.

Habitat Protection

Undoubtedly for most species, habitat destruction and degradation is among the most important factors in the decline of a majority of wildlife species other than the predators. Even the otter has probably been more affected by river pollution and habitat destruction than by hunting: hunting was just the final nail in its coffin.

Of all Britain's mammals, the bats are undoubtedly the species most seriously at risk at present. There are over a dozen species known in the British Isles, and there is little doubt that they are all declining rapidly. In addition to poisoning via eating contaminated insects, much of their woodland habitat has been destroyed, and they are also very sensitive to disturbance. Bats hibernate, and if they are disturbed during hibernation they have to burn valuable fat reserves. The cavernicolous (cave-dwelling) species, in particular, have suffered from disturbance by caving enthusiasts and even bat biologists—although, in fairness, it should be said that the latter discovered the problem of disturbance and led the fight to protect bats. Finally, in recent years the cold, wet springs and summers have had a disastrous effect on the breeding of most populations of bats.

Just as bats are an example of an acute conservation problem, they are also an example of what can be done to help endangered species. Many species of bat roost in caves and mines, and have been subjected to disturbance. By putting metal grilles over the entrances, which restricts the entry of humans but allows the bats free access, the protection of cave roosts is relatively straightforward. Many species have also adapted to man-made environments such as attics, cellars, church belfries, etc. By an intensive education programme it is often possible to convert people from antagonism towards bats to actively supporting measures to encourage and protect them. In addition, bats adapt to roosting in 'bat-boxes', particularly in summer. These are very like bird-boxes but, instead of a hole, they have narrow slit openings on the underside.

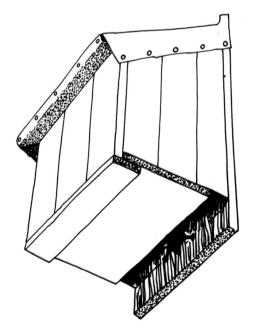

A bat-box.

A number of other mammals have been known to utilise bird-boxes, including pygmy shrews (quite high in trees), dormice, wood-mice, bank voles and weasels. Other types of artificial nesting sites can be created for many species: it is well known that hedgehogs will often

44

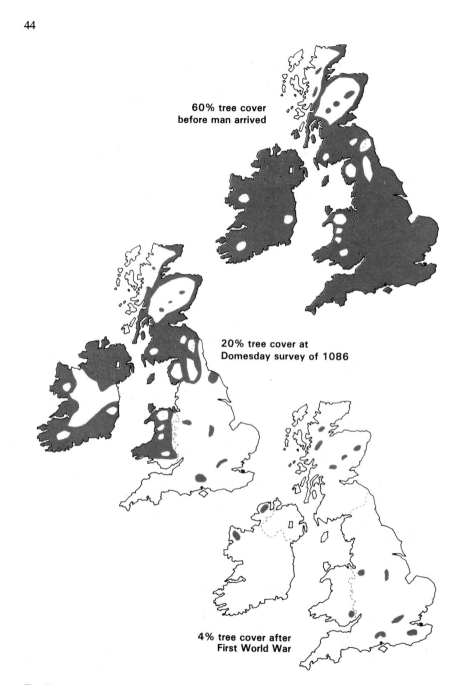

60% tree cover
before man arrived

20% tree cover at
Domesday survey of 1086

4% tree cover after
First World War

The disappearance of the woodland habitat of the British Isles.

build their breeding nests and hibernate in compost heaps; game-keepers often build cairns of stones to attract weasels and stoats (though their purpose is to trap and destroy them!); dormice and squirrels will nest in suitably sited boxes and, of course, a large number of animals—including badgers, foxes and deer—can be attracted to bait, water and saltlicks.

These are all artificial aids for conserving wild mammals. The most important factor is suitable habitat. As discussed elsewhere, most of Britain's native mammals are characteristic of woodlands or woodland edges. The natural woodlands of Britain have almost totally disappeared, with only scattered remnants or secondary plantations remaining. The woodland-edge habitat survives most extensively in the form of hedgerows—but even these are disappearing at an alarming rate. It is in the hedgerows that the majority of Britain's smaller mammals find a place to live, and it is upon these smaller mammals that many of the birds of prey depend.

Natural History and Conservation Societies

Since Charles Waterton, the eccentric eighteenth-century naturalist, put aside his estate for wildlife, more and more tracts of land have been dedicated as nature reserves. However, even before Waterton, game preserves were widespread and, until comparatively recently, the wardens of some bird reserves treated mammals little different to gamekeepers—weasels, stoats, squirrels and other mammals were animals which might kill birds or take their eggs. A more enlightened attitude now prevails.

In the early part of this century the nature protection and conservation movement got underway, and by the early 1950s 'County Trusts' were springing up all over the country and acquiring land. The formation of the Nature Conservancy (now the Nature Conservancy Council) in 1949 and the subsequent designation of Sites of Special Scientific Interest (SSSIs) and National Nature Reserves (NNRs) undoubtedly gave added impetus. Then, in the 1960s, the establishment of the World Wildlife Fund (British National Appeal) gave additional funding support to many local and national bodies for land purchase.

The following is a selection of organisations which are concerned with natural history or conservation or, in many cases, both.

Local and Regional Organisations

Local Natural History Societies
Most parts of Britain have at least one local natural history society (NHS), usually covering a county or an urban or more local area. They usually have their headquarters in libraries or museums and are often the depository for distribution records of mammals and other wildlife. For information on your local NHS, contact your local library or museum, or the Council for Environmental Conservation (CoEnCo), c/o London Zoo, Regent's Park, London NW1 4RY.

County Trusts for Nature Conservation
The Royal Society for Nature Conservation (RSNC), formerly the

Society for the Promotion of Nature Conservation, is the co-ordinating body for the County Trusts which cover most parts of Great Britain; Northern Ireland and Wales are covered by single Trusts, but most parts of England have a Trust for each county or a small number of counties. The Trusts own land and also manage privately owned land, and anyone interested in the conservation of mammals or any other wildlife should take an active interest in their local Country Trust; members usually have access to certain of their Trust reserves. There is also a junior branch of the RSNC—WATCH—which organises activities for eight–fifteen year olds. The RSNC will be able to tell you which is your local Trust.
RSNC, The Green, Nettleham, Lincolnshire LN2 2NR.

National Societies

There are a number of national bodies dealing with the conservation of mammals. The most relevant are:

The Mammal Society, Harvest House, London Road, Reading, Berkshire.
The leading specialist society, it publishes *Mammal Review, The Mammal Society Bulletin*, etc., and organises symposia and conferences. It also has specialist groups such as those concentrating on badgers and on bats.

World Wildlife Fund (British National Appeal), Panda House, 29 Greville Street, London EC1N 8AX.
This is part of an international fund-raising network, closely connected with the International Union for Conservation of Nature and Natural Resources (IUCN). It gives significant support to land purchase and makes other conservation grants in the United Kingdom.

Irish Wildlife Federation, 8 Westland Row, Dublin 2.
A relatively new body concerned with all aspects of wildlife, including mammals, in the Republic of Ireland.

Fauna and Flora Preservation Society, c/o Zoological Society of London, Regent's Park, London NW1 4RY.
An international society, the FFPS publishes a journal, *Oryx*, which carries articles on endangered species, including those in the British Isles. The FFPS is also involved with the Otter Haven Project and the British Bat Conservation Project.

British Deer Society, The Mill House, Bishopstrow, Warminster, Wiltshire.
A specialist society, its membership includes biologists and hunters; it also publishes a journal.

The Otter Trust, Earsham, near Bungay, Suffolk.
The Trust is concerned with all otters, particularly captive breeding, and it is engaged in breeding European otters.

Royal Society for the Prevention of Cruelty to Animals, The Causeway, Horsham, Sussex.
Through its Wild Animals Advisory Committee, the RSPCA maintains an interest in British mammals, but is mainly concerned with welfare issues such as those involving hunting and the use of gin traps and snares.

British Trust for Conservation Volunteers, c/o Zoological Society of London, Regent's Park, London NW1 4RY.
For young people interested in practical work on nature reserves.

The Mammal Species of the British Isles

The following maps are mainly based on those produced by Henry Arnold for the Biological Records Centre which plot known distribution on a 10-kilometre grid. However, considerable care has to be taken when interpreting any map since, among many other biases, they always tend to plot the distribution of observers rather than that of the species observed! Wherever possible I have tried to indicate possible changes in range; however, as it is only in the last few decades that records have been kept systematically on a national scale, the maps for historical distribution are often rather generalised. All the maps only indicate range; they do not indicate density.

The maps for bats are particularly problematical since bats are rarely identified accurately, and the records used to compile distribution maps come from a wide time span. Furthermore, since many bat species have declined, particularly since 1950, the maps may tend to give too large an area for present-day range.

The maps for cetaceans were also a problem: whales, dolphins and porpoises can (and occasionally do) turn up in practically all coastal waters. Until recently there has been very little organised collection of field observations of cetaceans, and so the maps merely indicate the areas where cetaceans are likely to be encountered, based on strandings as well as sight records.

All measurements on the following pages are given in their original form, with an approximate conversion into imperial (or, occasionally, metric) in brackets. Imperial measurements are rarely used by biologists but, where older sources have used the imperial (notably for land areas), these measurements have been given in their original form, with the metric equivalent in brackets. The figures are all approximate, and are often averages. For an accurate range of measurements, the *Handbook of British Mammals* (*see* page 38) should be consulted.

To use the maps:

■ Present distribution

Other types of distribution—past, that of a related species, relative density, etc.—are indicated on individual maps.

Hedgehog

Erinaceus europaeus

Size: up to 26 cm (10¼ in); tail concealed.

Description: distinctive spiny body, which rolls into a ball when alarmed, presenting the finder with a mass of spines. Young are soft spined.

Behaviour & breeding: make nests of leaves and grass in wood piles, etc. in which 2–9 young are born in summer; occasionally a second litter later. Normally nocturnal and hibernate.

Tracks or signs: are noisy and their snuffling and shuffling through undergrowth is distinctive. Nests found in tree roots, compost heaps, log piles, etc.

Food: insects and almost any other invertebrates and small animals.

In Britain, hedgehogs are widely distributed, but absent from most Scottish islands; the populations that do occur on small islands are mostly known to be the result of re-introductions. They are also present over most of Europe, except the far north. Found in a wide variety of mainly woodland habitats, they are often particularly abundant in suburban gardens and parks. They are surprisingly agile, climb well and swim. In the past they were persecuted by gamekeepers for their alleged depredations on the eggs of gamebirds. The decrease in gamekeepering has probably allowed hedgehog populations to increase in some areas, and because of their appetite for garden pests, they are more usually regarded as beneficial now. The hedgehog has few natural enemies (foxes and badgers do kill them), but man, and particularly motor vehicles, kill large numbers.

Common Shrew

Sorex araneus

Size: up to 8.5 cm ($3\frac{1}{4}$ in) plus tail of up to 5.5 cm ($2\frac{1}{4}$ in).

Description: rather mouse-like, but with pointed snout; dark velvety fur and very small eyes.

Behaviour & breeding: active for periods of up to 10 hours interspersed with shorter periods of rest. Breeds March to October; females may have 2 litters of up to 8 young, which leave the nest after about 24 days; mature the same year.

Tracks or signs: high-pitched squeaking often heard in hedgerows. Remains (red-toothed mandibles) often common in pellets of birds of prey.

Food: mainly insects, worms and other invertebrates.

One of the most abundant small mammals in Britain, the common shrew is widespread in the British Isles, but absent from Ireland and most islands; it also occurs in most of northern, central and eastern Europe. It has recently been discovered that there are several species of 'common' shrews, all very similar, but with chromosome differences. The common shrew is found in a wide range of habitats up to about 100 m (3300 ft), but is most abundant in well-wooded habitats and other habitats with dense grass, bracken and other ground cover. It makes runways, and also uses the burrows of others such as voles, mice and moles. Populations of common shrews fluctuate widely from place to place and year to year. Most of the adult generations in any year die in late summer or early autumn after breeding, and the only animals to survive the winter are young ones.

Pygmy Shrew

Sorex minutus

Size: up to 6 cm (2¼ in), plus tail of up to 6.8 cm (2¾ in).

Description: very small, with proportionally long tail. Rather mouse-like but with pointed snout and velvety fur.

Behaviour & breeding: live in runs and burrows of other mammals, usually hidden by vegetation. Aggressive, and frequently heard squeaking. Litter of 2–8 young, born in an underground nest; probably 2 litters a year between April and August.

Tracks or signs: bones found in pellets and faeces of predators.

Food: mainly insects and other invertebrates, particularly woodlice.

The pygmy shrew is probably the most widely distributed mammal in Britain, and is found in almost all habitats from sea level to the top of Ben Nevis. It is widespread in most of Europe except southern Spain and Portugal. They often occur in more open habitats and usually have less dense populations than the common shrew. Like the latter, it is one of the most important prey items for a wide variety of bird and mammal predators. The pygmy shrew is usually absent from city centres, but often found in the larger suburban parks and commons, and along railway embankments. Relatively little is known about how the populations are controlled; the relative abundance of food may affect the number of females breeding in the same year as they are born and predators may be important. However, some predators such as domestic cats find them unpalatable.

Water Shrew

Neomys fodiens

Size: total length of 14 cm (5½ in) of which tail is just under half.

Description: black above and usually white below, but can be darker or uniformly dark all over. Appears silvery under water.

Behaviour & breeding: swims with alternate limb-strokes; walks on bottom. Breeds mid-April to September with peak in early summer; gestation of 24 days, 3–8 young in litter, weaned at 4–5 weeks. Usually 2 litters annually.

Tracks or signs: can be heard squeaking in dense vegetation by waterside. Remains found in bird-of-prey pellets.

Food: wide variety of small animals, including fish and frogs, but mainly invertebrates. Saliva contains venom.

The water shrew is widespread in England, Scotland and Wales but absent from most islands, as well as Ireland. In the north it is much more sparsely distributed, but it may have been overlooked on many islands. In Europe it is widespread from Scandinavia, east to the USSR and south to the Pyrenees, Italy and southern Yugoslavia. Water shrews are found in a wide variety of habitats, particularly those close to rivers, streams, lakes, ponds and marshes (watercress beds are favoured); they are also often found a considerable distance from water. It is the least abundant and least widespread of the British shrews, but cannot be considered rare. Although there is little data, it is probable that the water shrew has declined drastically in many areas as a result of land drainage and water pollution. The venom in its saliva is used to paralyse prey.

Mole

Talpa europaea

Tumps (mole-hills).

Size: up to 15 cm (6 in); tail very short.

Description: dense velvety black fur, pointed snout, enlarged forelimbs, eyes tiny but visible.

Behaviour & breeding: active intermittently during the day and night. Breeding season is short, commencing in late February, with a gestation period of 4 weeks. Young born in underground nests, often in a large mole-hill (fortress). Young are weaned at 4–5 weeks; breed the following year.

Tracks or signs: mole-hills (tumps) and surface runs.

Food: mainly worms, but also other invertebrates.

The mole is widespread in England, Scotland (where its range may have increased in the past 200 years) and Wales, but absent from Ireland and many islands. It is also present over most of continental Europe. It is found in a variety of mainly wooded habitats, and also in open pastures, meadows and hill country, wherever there is sufficient soil for it to tunnel. It spends almost its entire life underground, usually only found on the surface during flooding or extreme drought. The young disperse from the nests into poorer habitats and often make shallow burrows, exposed to predators. Although the habitat is suitable, most moles have been exterminated in parks and gardens, particularly in towns, because of their tunnelling activities. In rural areas moles are still trapped, though not as extensively as in the past, and are generally abundant.

Whiskered Bat

Myotis mystacinus

Size: head and body 3.5–4.8 cm ($1\frac{1}{4}$–2 in); wingspan up to 24 cm ($9\frac{1}{2}$ in).

Description: very small. Upper parts dark grey, underside whitish; wings, face and ears very dark.

Behaviour & breeding: nocturnal; emerges around sunset. Roosts in trees and buildings and sometimes in caves and mines in winter. Single young each year; may mature at 3 months, normally at 15 months. Maximum lifespan recorded 19.5 years; average 4.

Flight: fluttering, often along hedges.

Food: small insects, spiders, etc.

Brandt's bat (*Myotis brandti*): distinguishable from whiskered bat only by examination in the hand by an expert.

Brandt's bat.

The whiskered bat is widespread in England, Wales and Ireland, and also on the Continent; its exact distribution is poorly known because of its confusion with Brandt's bat (*see below*). Studies of whiskered bats hibernating in caves in Europe have shown that there are usually more males than females. Like most other species of bats, the greatest mortalities (after the initial infant and juvenile mortalities) occur during hibernation, with only about three-quarters of adults surviving each year. Among the causes of death recorded is predation by shrews and mice in the hibernacula. Along with other bats, this species has probably suffered declines due to hedgerow and woodland clearance, and the effects of pesticides. Brandt's bat has recently been recognised in Britain, and its exact distribution and relationship with the whiskered bat has yet to be worked out.

Natterer's Bat

Myotis nattereri

Size: head and body 4.0–5.5 cm (1½–2¼ in); wingspan up to 30 cm (11¾ in).

Description: medium-sized bat; light brownish above, whitish below with pale muzzle and ears. Characteristic fringe of hairs on edge of tail membrane.

Behaviour & breeding: nocturnal. Found in parkland, woodland, etc.; roosts in trees, buildings and caves, etc. Mostly solitary, but females form nursery colonies. Single offspring born June–July. Maximum life recorded is 12 years.

Flight: fairly slow, but fluttering.

Food: insects, mostly captured in flight, but also picked off foliage.

Daubenton's bat (*Myotis daubentoni*) differs: slightly smaller wingspan; generally darker; rather large feet.

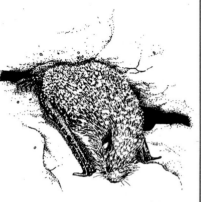
Daubenton's bat.

Natterer's bat is widely distributed throughout Ireland and Britain as far north as Scotland; although there are relatively few positive records from Ireland, it is probably widespread. It also occurs throughout Europe and eastwards through Asia to Japan. During hibernation, they show a preference for the cool sites around the entrances to caves. Like other bats in the British Isles, they have probably declined in many areas with the destruction of hedgerows and the elimination of insects with pesticides and other major changes to the woodland environment, particularly the loss of mature deciduous woodland. Daubenton's bat is often associated with water and has been recorded snatching small fish from the water's surface. The females often form large nursery colonies in buildings; in winter they often roost in caves or crevices, or hang free.

Daubenton's bat

Common Long-eared Bat

Plecotus auritus

Size: head and body 3.7–4.8 cm ($1\frac{1}{2}$–2 in); wingspan up to 28.5 cm ($11\frac{1}{4}$ in).

Description: small, usually buffish above, paler below; wings thin and translucent. Easily recognised by exceptionally large ears.

Behaviour & breeding: nocturnal; usually emerges after sunset. Males mature at 12 months, females later; single young is born mid to late summer. Hibernates in trees and buildings, and occasionally caves; often uses bat-boxes.

Flight: fluttering and hovering, often picking insects off foliage.

Food: insects, spiders, etc.; nocturnal moths form main diet in summer.

Grey long-eared bat (*Plecotus austriacus*) differs: greyer; slightly larger; other anatomical differences.

Grey long-eared bat.

The common long-eared bat is widespread throughout Ireland and Britain, except for the north of Scotland and western islands; it also occurs eastwards through Europe and Asia to Japan. It is often resident, occupying the same roost throughout most of the year. However, long-eared bats have also been seen from a boat 72 km (45 miles) off the Yorkshire coast; the bats were coming from the north-east and later continuing towards England. There are also records of them from light-ships, off the east coast of Britain and also off Ireland. They are occasionally killed by cats and owls. The grey long-eared bat was first recognised as being present as recently as 1963. Although widespread on the Continent, its range in Britain is confined to a small area on the south coast of England; it may, however, be found elsewhere in the future.

Grey long-eared bat

Bechstein's Bat

Myotis bechsteini

Size: head and body 4.3–5.0 cm (1¾–2 in); wingspan up to 30 cm (11¾ in).

Description: medium-sized; pale brown above, pale below; ears and wings dark brownish; ears very large—up to 2.6 cm (1 in).

Behaviour & breeding: nocturnal; emerges shortly after sunset. Hibernates in caves, cellars, roofs, etc. Little known about breeding, but small nursery colonies formed in hollow trees. Males usually solitary.

Flight: slow and usually rather low.

Food: mostly moths, taken both on the wing and picked off leaves.

Mouse-eared bat (*Myotis myotis*) differs: length to 8 cm (3¼ in); wingspan to 45 cm (17¾ in); pinkish muzzle.

Mouse-eared bat.

Bechstein's bat is one of Britain's rarer and least known species, confined to south-east Wales and central southern England; it also occurs in Europe as far east as the Caucasus, but is scarce in most places. It is primarily a forest species and its present-day range is probably very much more restricted than in the past when most of Europe was covered in deciduous forest. Evidence for this comes from Grimes Graves (chalk mines) in Norfolk where large numbers of bones of Bechstein's bats have been found; at the time the mines were in use (3000–4000 years ago), Britain was still extensively forested. The mouse-eared bat was discovered in southern England in 1956 (there are also two nineteenth-century records), but although protected by law since 1973, it is now on the verge of extinction. It will fly up to 200 km (125 miles) between winter and summer roosts.

c. 1900

Barbastelle

Barbastella barbastellus

Size: head and body 4.0–5.2 cm ($1\frac{1}{2}$–2 in); wingspan up to 28 cm (11 in).

Description: medium-sized bat; dark brown above, slightly paler below. Fur has pale tips, giving characteristic 'frosted' appearance. Face, ears, wings blackish; ears long and broad, meeting over the head.

Behaviour & breeding: nocturnal; may emerge before sunset and is often active throughout the night. Roosts in buildings, tree-holes and caves. Is migratory in continental Europe, but movements not known in Britain. Females form nursery colonies; males solitary. Little is known of breeding.

Flight: low and fluttering, often over water.

Food: insects.

The barbastelle is one of Britain's lesser-known species, which has only rarely been found, usually in wooded river valleys. It is also found throughout western and central Europe—where large concentrations are sometimes discovered during hibernation and cold spells—eastwards to central Russia. The relatively few records of this species in Britain suggest that its range may have contracted within the last 100 years or so. In 1976, about half of the total number of observations of this bat related to 1900–1959, and only a third to post-1960; the rest were pre-1900. Most sightings are from a line joining the Severn estuary and Sunderland, with a majority in central-southern and south-west England; it may now be extinct in Wales, and is certainly much sparcer in the east of its range. Its decline may have been in progress for many centuries.

? Probably present, but declining

Pipistrelle

Pipistrellus pipistrellus

Size: head and body 3.5–4.5 cm ($1\frac{1}{4}$–$1\frac{3}{4}$ in); wingspan up to 25 cm ($9\frac{3}{4}$ in).

Description: very small. Colour variable, but generally medium-dark brownish above, paler below; ears and muzzle dark. Ears short, rounded and brown.

Behaviour & breeding: nocturnal; usually emerges shortly after sunset. Forms large nursery colonies (up to 1000). Single young (occasionally twins) born from late June through July, after gestation of about 44 days. Maximum recorded life is 11 years.

Flight: fast and erratic.

Food: wide variety of insects.

Nathusius' pipistrelle (*Pipistrellus nathusisi*) differs: slightly larger; fur with pale tips, giving 'frosted' appearance.

The pipistrelle is the most widespread and abundant bat in Britain and Ireland, occurring in all parts except very exposed uplands and islands; it is present throughout Europe eastwards to Kashmir. It occurs in all but the most heavily built-up parts of towns. In the British Isles and western Europe, it roosts mainly in buildings and trees and only rarely in caves and mines; in eastern Europe large roosts (up to 100 000) have been found in caves. The longest movement recorded in Britain was one killed by a cat 69 km (43 miles) from the place where it had been ringed 11 years before. The pipistrelle probably declined in rural areas during the 1960s with the widespread and often indiscriminate use of DDT and other organochlorines. Nathusius' pipistrelle has been recorded once (1969) in Britain. It is very similar to the pipistrelle and could easily be overlooked.

Noctule

Nyctalus noctula

Size: head and body 7.0–8.2 cm (2¾–3¼ in); wingspan up to 39 cm (15¼ in).

Description: large; upper parts tawny, underside sometimes slightly paler; face, ears and wings dark. Ears rounded and short with very small tragus.

Behaviour & breeding: nocturnal, but often emerges before sunset, and may fly by day. Single young sometimes born June–July, usually in tree-hole.

Flight: high and direct with 'corkscrew' dives. Voice in flight often audible.

Food: large insects, caught and eaten on wing.

Lesser noctule (*Nyctalus leisleri*) differs: length to 6.4 cm (2½ in); wingspan to 34 cm (13½ in).

Lesser noctule (Leisler's bat).

The noctule is widespread and locally abundant in England and Wales, but absent from Ireland and most of Scotland (although there are some old records of them there). It also occurs throughout Europe and northern Asia. It is primarily a woodland species, but has adapted to a wide variety of habitats and is often found in parks and in suburban areas. It roosts mainly in tree-holes where, on hot summer days, its loud squeaking can be heard. Birds such as starlings compete with noctules and often drive them out of roosting holes, and the clearing of dead timber and the general disappearance of woodland has undoubtedly affected their numbers and distribution. The lesser noctule (or Leisler's bat) is similar to the noctule, but smaller. Although widespread in Ireland, its range in Britain is restricted to southern England and Wales.

Lesser noctule

Serotine

Eptesicus serotinus

Size: head and body 6.0–7.5 cm (2¼–3 in); wingspan up to 38 cm (15 in).

Description: large bat; dark brown above, underparts paler. Moderately bony, rounded ears. Distinctive swollen muzzle.

Behaviour & breeding: nocturnal, usually emerging about 15 minutes after sunset, but very variable. In summer, females gather in large nursery colonies in roofs or trees; males usually solitary. Often found near human habitation; in summer, are found in lofts, and in winter in cracks in masonry and in cellars.

Flight: fairly level, often high, with occasional swoops.

Food: mainly flying insects.

The serotine is confined to England approximately south of a line from the Wash to the Severn, and has not been recorded from Wales, Cornwall, Scotland or Ireland. It is widespread in Europe as far north as Denmark. Within its British range, its distribution is patchy, despite it having adapted to roosting in buildings—both in summer and in winter. In its winter roosts it appears to prefer colder sites such as cave entrances, and in Poland it has been recorded at temperatures of –6°C (21.2°F). In Britain it is rarely found in caves, generally staying in open wooded country, and its uneven distribution may be associated with habitat requirements. Like most other bats, it has probably suffered from pesticides and the destruction of roosting-sites with the clearance of old timber resulting from the spread of Dutch elm disease.

? Probably present but declining

Greater Horseshoe Bat

Rhinolophus ferrumequinum

Size: head and body 5.6–6.8 cm ($2\frac{1}{4}$–$2\frac{3}{4}$ in); wingspan up to 39 cm ($15\frac{1}{4}$ in).

Description: large; easily recognised by distinctive horseshoe-shaped nose-leaf (skin involved in production of ultra-sonic pulses for echo location).

Behaviour & breeding: nocturnal; usually emerges 30 minutes after sunset and is active throughout night. Roosts alone or in large clusters, sleeping suspended with wings wrapped around body. Single young born June–August. Start flying at 22 days. Normally reach maturity at 3 years.

Flight: rather slow fluttering and butterfly-like.

Food: mainly flying insects.

The greater horseshoe bat is now restricted to a small area in the south-west of Britain. It is also present in continental Europe, eastwards through Asia to the Himalayas and Japan, and in north Africa. It is now one of Britain's rarest bats, although at the turn of the century it was still widespread in southern England, with colonies numbering several hundreds. In the summer they roost mainly in belfries, roof spaces and barns, and in winter in old mines, caves and cellars. Since the turn of the century their range has contracted, until there are no more than three main populations, their numbers having been reduced to about 800 by 1973. The decline has continued and can probably be attributed to a number of factors including human disturbance of the roosts, and the effect of bad summers on breeding success. It has been protected since 1973.

c. 1880

Lesser Horseshoe Bat

Rhinolophus hipposideros

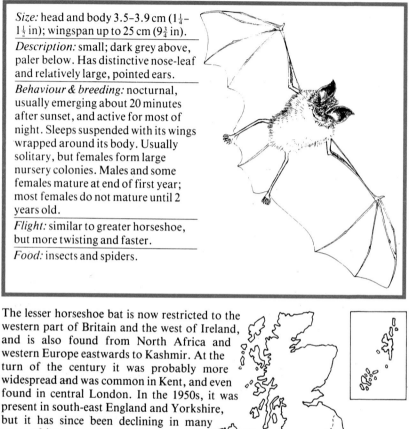

Size: head and body 3.5–3.9 cm (1¼–1½ in); wingspan up to 25 cm (9¾ in).

Description: small; dark grey above, paler below. Has distinctive nose-leaf and relatively large, pointed ears.

Behaviour & breeding: nocturnal, usually emerging about 20 minutes after sunset, and active for most of night. Sleeps suspended with its wings wrapped around its body. Usually solitary, but females form large nursery colonies. Males and some females mature at end of first year; most females do not mature until 2 years old.

Flight: similar to greater horseshoe, but more twisting and faster.

Food: insects and spiders.

The lesser horseshoe bat is now restricted to the western part of Britain and the west of Ireland, and is also found from North Africa and western Europe eastwards to Kashmir. At the turn of the century it was probably more widespread and was common in Kent, and even found in central London. In the 1950s, it was present in south-east England and Yorkshire, but it has since been declining in many parts of its range. The British population was previously described *as Rhinolophus hipposideros minutus* but it has been shown that this subspecies forms part of a cline, with the bats of Britain and France being the smallest, gradually increasing in size eastwards to Romania. They are found mainly in woodland habitats, roosting in caves, cellars and mines, hanging free, usually singly, fairly low down. In summer they also roost in roofs and barns.

c. 1900

Brown Hare

Lepus capensis

Size: up to about 65 cm (25½ in).

Description: yellowish-brown with long, black-tipped ears, and short, black and white tail.

Behaviour & breeding: mainly active at night, but also frequently seen by day. Usually solitary outside the breeding season, when males gather and fight and pursue females ('Mad March hares'). 2–4 young (leverets) born in a hollow 'form' in the open.

Tracks or signs: leave few signs, but footprints are distinctive. 'Form' is a depression usually against a tussock or hedge, but sometimes quite exposed.

Food: mainly herbage, particularly grass; also cereal crops, turnips and bark.

Brown hares are widespread over most of England, Scotland and Wales, and have been introduced into Ireland as well as into the Hebrides, the Isle of Man, Orkney and Shetland (where it has subsequently died out). They occur widely in Europe, Asia and Africa, and are one of the most widely distributed land animals in the world. They are most common in farmland and are particularly abundant in pasture, woodlands, marshes and other habitats up to an altitude of about 500 m (1640 ft). The populations fluctuate enormously. They are sometimes serious pests of agriculture, but are also regarded as game animals and are subject to protection under game laws. Although still widespread, the overall number have declined drastically in many parts of England and this is reflected in reduced game bags; the reasons for this is not understood.

Varying Hare

Lepus timidus

Size: up to a total length of 60 cm (23¼ in).

Description: greyish- or yellowish-brown in summer, and (except in Ireland) white with black ear-tips in winter.

Behaviour & breeding: active by day and night; may gather in large herds, particularly in winter. Breeding from February to July; 1–3 young per litter and up to 3 litters a year. Born in a form in a short burrow or rock cleft. The young do not breed until the following year. Whistle as an alarm call and scream when injured.

Tracks or signs: footprints are characteristic.

Food: grasses, heathers, sedges and other plants.

Also known as Arctic, mountain, blue or variable hare, originally it was confined to Ireland and the Scottish Highlands, but has been introduced widely into other parts of the British Isles. (*See* 1, 2, 3, 4 on map.) It currently survives in the Hebrides, Orkney, Shetland, the Peak District and the Isle of Man, but is rare or has died out in the Pennines and North Wales. It is also found in Iceland, Scandinavia, the Baltic states, the USSR and the Alps. In Scotland varying hares are confined to upland areas, usually open moorland and rocky hillsides from 300–900 m (1000–2900 ft), but come lower down in winter. In Ireland they are found in a wide variety of open habitats. The population density varies enormously from 1 or 2 to over 200 per 1000 acres (400 hectares). However, populations fluctuate widely from year to year. It can be a pest to agriculture.

Rabbit

Oryctolagus cuniculus

Size: up to about 45 cm (17¾ in); with short (less than 8 cm, 3¼ in) tail.

Description: ears long (up to 7 cm, 2¾ in) but are proportionally shorter than hares' and lack black tips.

Behaviour & breeding: live colonially, usually in extensive burrows, but occasionally above ground in dense vegetation. Breed mainly from January–June, but also all other times. Usually 4–6 young per litter, maturing at about 3 months.

Tracks or signs: tracks similar to brown hares'. Distinctive droppings often deposited on mole-hills or tussocks. Burrows often with closely grazed surroundings.

Food: wide range of grasses and herbage.

Droppings

Originally confined to north-west Africa and Iberia, the rabbit was first introduced into the British Isles by the Normans and is now widespread in a wide variety of habitats—from cultivated land to moorlands, sand dunes and woodlands—as well as on all the larger islands and many of the smaller ones around the coast. Since the arrival of myxomatosis in 1953 the population has become much smaller; prior to then, some 60–100 million were killed annually, and densities of 1 or 2 per acre (0.4 hectare) were common, sometimes rising to 15–20. Much of its pre-myxomatosis habitat has now become overgrown. After an initial heavy mortality in the year 1954/55 the rabbit and myxomatosis have now settled into a more or less balanced state, where the population builds up for several years, then crashes. In Britain they are serious agricultural pests.

Red Squirrel

Sciurus vulgaris

Drey

Size: up to 30 cm (11¾ in), of which tail is less than half.

Description: bushy tail; ear tufts which gradually bleach to almost white before each moult.

Behaviour & breeding: very agile; active by day, becoming inactive during bad weather. Builds nests (dreys). Two main breeding seasons (January–April and May–August) in south; only one in Scotland. 3–6 young in litter.

Tracks or signs: often makes pathways across clearings between trees; stripped cones are distinctive, also untidy dreys in tree forks.

Food: seeds of wide variety of trees, berries, fungi and other plant material; also eggs and nestlings. Stores food.

Although now widespread in Europe but only abundant in the coniferous woodlands of Scotland, the red squirrel was once found in almost all wooded habitats in the British Isles. It became extinct over most of Scotland in the late eighteenth and early nineteenth century, but was re-introduced and recolonised, and was introduced into Ireland in the nineteenth century. Between 1900 and 1930 it declined over most of its range in England and Wales, and the grey squirrel colonised much of the vacant habitat. From then until the mid-1940s it made a slight recovery; since then for reasons not fully understood, it has continued to decline in England and Wales, and is likely to become extinct over most of its range in the next few years. The British subspecies (*S.v. leucourus*) has a distinct pelage change—the tail and ear tufts bleach to almost white in spring.

Maximum range

Grey Squirrel

Sciurus carolinensis

Size: head and body up to 30 cm (11¾ in); tail up to 25 cm (9¾ in).

Description: slightly larger than red squirrel; normally grey, but can have rusty, reddish tinge. Lacks ear tufts.

Behaviour & breeding: active by day. Builds dreys (nests) and also uses tree-holes; even enters attics and lofts. Two breeding seasons: mating takes place December–January and May–June. Gestation about 7 weeks; 3–7 young per litter, weaned at about 10 weeks, sexually mature at 6–11 months.

Tracks or signs: remains of pine cones and nuts distinctive; untidy dreys in trees.

Food: nuts, berries, roots, fungi and other vegetable matter; also insects, eggs, etc.

Remains of spruce cone

The grey squirrel was introduced into Britain from North America from 1876 to 1929, at about 30 separate sites. It is now found in almost all woodland, parkland and suburban habitats in southern England and Wales, where it has replaced the less terrestrial, native red squirrel in most areas, despite campaigns to eliminate grey squirrels, and even the payment of bounties for tails (now ceased). It is more adaptable than the red squirrel, particularly in mixed and deciduous woodlands. In northern England, Scotland and Ireland it is more recently established, but rarely found in coniferous woodlands and forests. Population declines are usually associated with bad crops of acorns or beechmast, and bad winters; they hide food during the autumn. The grey squirrel damages trees and is hunted and trapped as a pest; in North America it is regarded as a game species.

1930

Bank Vole

Clethrionomys glareolus

Size: head and body from 8–11 cm
($3\frac{1}{4}$–$4\frac{1}{4}$ in), tail up to 6 cm ($2\frac{1}{4}$ in).

Description: reddish-brown back,
fairly long tail, and ears more
prominent than field vole.

Behaviour & breeding: lives mainly in
thick cover, but is also agile climber;
mainly diurnal. Makes burrows.
Occasionally enters houses and farm
buildings in winter. Breeding season
usually extends from mid-April to
September, but sometimes later. 4–5
litters, of up to about 6 young each
year.

Tracks or signs: characteristic stores
of nuts and berries under logs, etc.

Food: variety of vegetable matter
(roots, berries, nuts, fungi, etc.); diet
also includes animal matter (insects,
molluscs, etc.).

The bank vole is widespread in the British Isles
and found on many islands. It was first recorded in Ireland in 1964, a result of
introduction; since its discovery, its range
has been spreading. Subspecies occur on
some islands; that of Skomer Island, off the
coast of Wales, shows little fear of man. In continental Europe it is found from northern
Spain through France to eastern Europe
and Scandinavia. The bank vole occurs
in a wide variety of habitats, but is
particularly abundant in deciduous woodland, hedgerows
and parkland wherever there
is much dense undercover
of brambles, etc. Population
densities of 12–74 per hectare
($2\frac{1}{2}$ acres) and, on Skomer, 210
per hectare, have been re-
corded, and bank voles occasionally
become pests of forestry. They are an
important prey item for owls and other predators, particularly tawny owls and weasels.

1950

Field Vole

Microtus agrestis

Size: up to 13 cm (5 in), plus tail of up to 4.5 cm ($1\frac{3}{4}$ in).

Description: mouse-like but blunter muzzle, shorter tail and ears largely concealed; greyish brown.

Behaviour & breeding: active by day and night. Breeding season is mainly March–September; up to 8 young per litter which are weaned between 3–6 weeks and become sexually mature between 3–6 weeks later.

Tracks or signs: extensive runs and burrows in dense herbage. Remains very common in bird-of-prey pellets.

Food: mainly grasses; also bulbs, roots and bark; occasionally insects, molluscs and other invertebrates.

Orkney vole (*M. arvalis*): only minor differences; occurs as introduction (probably by Vikings) in Orkney.

The field vole (also called the short-tailed vole) is found 'throughout northern Europe from north-west Spain to the USSR, in mainly open, grassy habitats with dense ground cover, including pasture, meadows, moors and hedgerows at almost all altitudes in Britain. It is absent from Ireland, but found on many islands where separate subspecies have been described (*see* p. 20). Field vole populations are subject to extremely wide fluctuations, usually with 3–4 year cycles. They are one of the most numerous British mammals, and densities can range from almost none to hundreds per hectare ($2\frac{1}{2}$ acres), and these 'plagues' are then invariably followed by dramatic crashes in population. They are one of the main foods of foxes, and some predators often increase in numbers as vole population increases. Field voles are sometimes serious agricultural pests.

Water Vole

Arvicola terrestris

Size: head and body up to 20 cm (7¾ in), tail up to 13 cm (5 in).

Description: like a small, blunt-headed, short-tailed rat.

Behaviour & breeding: active by day and night; often shows little fear of man. Nests in burrows or among reeds and grasses. 3–6 young, born April–October.

Tracks or signs: runs and entrances to burrows along river banks; on land, may make earth 'hills'.

Food: mainly grasses, reeds and other vegetable matter; occasionally animals including molluscs and carrion.

Coypu (*Myocastor coypus*): largest rodent in England; length up to 110 cm (43¼ in), of which tail is half; weight up to 9 kg (20 lb).

The water vole is found throughout northern Europe, and although most abundant in marshes, rivers and other aquatic habitats, it is often found at a considerable distance from water. It does not occur in Ireland or on most islands, and may be decreasing in Britain. The populations of water voles fluctuate widely, but rarely increase to a level where they do much damage; occasionally their burrows undermine banks and they attack crops. The coypu is the vole's giant relative from South America, which has escaped from fur farms and now lives ferally in East Anglia. It does considerable damage, and after extensive campaigns by the Ministry of Agriculture their populations have been contained within fairly limited areas. They primarily eat aquatic plants but will sometimes raid crops such as sugar beets.

Coypu: 1980
Coypu: scattered introductions 1930 on

Black Rat

Rattus rattus

Size: up to a total length of about 45 cm (17¾ in) of which the tail is just over half.

Description: generally blackish, but rather variable; can often be brownish and confused with brown rat. Tail long, ears prominent.

Behaviour & breeding: mainly nocturnal, generally gregarious. Breeds throughout year, with 3–5 litters of up to 10 young, maturing at about 4 months.

Tracks or signs: spoils stored food; droppings, gnawings and other damage and odour all characteristic.

Food: opportunist, eating almost anything with any nutritional value, particularly cereal grains.

(a) gnawed snail shell; (b) oats; (c) droppings.

During the Middle Ages, black rats spread to Britain from India, via continental Europe, and were the carriers of plagues such as the Black Death. Since the arrival of the brown rat in Britain in the late eighteenth century, the black rat has disappeared except from areas around ports, a few city centres and from the island of Lundy off Devon. In most of northern Europe it has undergone a similar decline, and it is probable that most populations are maintained by immigration from ships coming from the tropics. It can survive in a wide variety of habitats, but shows a marked preference for man-made environments and also is less terrestrial than the brown rat, often occurring in the upper part of buildings. In Europe, at least locally, the black rat can be considered vulnerable or even endangered, but everywhere its legal status is that of a pest.

Brown Rat

Rattus norvegicus

Size: up to a total of 50 cm (19¾ in), of which tail is less than half.

Description: generally brownish, paler on underside but very variable; fur rather shaggy; thick scaly tail.

Behaviour & breeding: usually nocturnal, and sociable; an excellent swimmer. Often associated with man and his domestic animals. Breeds all year round with 3–5 litters of up to 12 young, which leave the nest at 3 weeks, maturing at about 3 months; the females defend young very aggressively.

Tracks or signs: often cause extensive damage to stored food and property. Droppings, gnawings and greasy runways all characteristic.

Food: opportunistic; almost anything edible, but prefers cereals.

(a) greasy runway; (b) food remains; (c) droppings.

The brown rat (also called the common rat) originated in the Far East, but is now virtually cosmopolitan, having spread as far as the Antarctic (South Georgia) and Arctic Alaska, and is found alongside man in many parts of the world, particularly in coastal areas. It occurs throughout the British Isles and is probably only absent from very small, uninhabited islands. It lives in a wide variety of habitats, mainly connected with buildings, rubbish tips, farms, sewers, but particularly in summer, spreading throughout the countryside. It is one of the most serious mammal pests, damaging enormous quantities of stored food and property; a single straw rick can harbour up to 500 or more rats. Brown rats (especially young ones) are important prey for many other species, including barn owls, stoats and foxes. Domesticated brown rats are important laboratory animals.

House Mouse

Mus musculus

Size: head and body up to about 10 cm (4 in) with tail of about equal length.

Description: colour variable, but generally grey or grey-brown above, paler grey below. Those living in agricultural areas are usually smaller and browner.

Behaviour & breeding: mainly nocturnal, but also active by day; high-pitched squeak often heard. Breeding is continuous throughout the year, with up to about 10 litters a year of 4–8 young which are weaned at 18 days and breed at 6 weeks.

Tracks or signs: often spoil food, leaving droppings; characteristic odour; distinctive holes in skirting boards, etc.

Food: opportunistic; almost anything edible, preference for cereals.

House mice originated in Central Asia, but spread across Europe some 2000 years ago, reaching Britain probably before A D 300; they are now found in almost all parts of the world, wherever there are human habitations. In Britain the house mouse occurs on all in-habited islands, but on few if any uninhabited ones; a distinctive subspecies (*M.m. muralis*) formerly occurred on the Scottish island of St Kilda but became extinct shortly after the human population was evacuated from the island in 1930, probably because the house mouse was unable to compete with the wood mouse. House mice live both in towns and in the countryside, and have even been found living in meat cold stores; in ricks the density can reach as high as 15 per cubic metre (1.3 cu. yd). They are major pests, and when left undisturbed can rapidly build up to plague proportions.

Harvest Mouse

Micromys minutus

Size: head and body to about 8 cm ($3\frac{1}{4}$ in), plus slightly shorter tail.

Description: reddish-brown upper parts, white beneath; tail prehensile.

Behaviour & breeding: active by day and night. Builds characteristic cricket-ball-sized summer nest of woven grass and stems, usually 20–50 cm ($7\frac{3}{4}$–$19\frac{3}{4}$ in) above ground in dense herbage. Several litters of up to 6 young; leave the nest at about 15 days. In winter they live mainly at ground level or below ground. Habitat is specialised: lives among stems of reeds, cereals, weeds, etc.

Tracks or signs: in winter, summer nests are often clearly visible in hedgerows, reedbeds, etc.

Food: variety of vegetable matter; also insects.

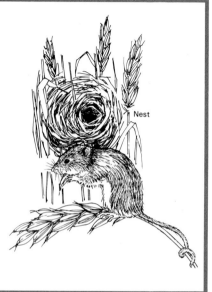

Nest

The harvest mouse is widespread in Europe, but absent from most of Scandinavia, and from Mediterranean Europe. In the British Isles, where it is the smallest rodent, it is absent from Ireland and most islands, scarce in Wales and found only in the south-east of Scotland, but in England it is widespread and locally abundant. The first accurate description of it in Britain was by Gilbert White in 1767, when it was abundant in cornfields and in thistles. It has been traditionally associated with cornfields and other cereals and, with the mechanisation of farming, was believed to have declined and may have actually decreased in numbers in some areas. However, recent surveys have shown it to be widespread in habitats other than cereal crops; favoured are hedgerows with long grass, marshes and the edges of reedbeds. Up to 200 per hectare ($2\frac{1}{2}$ acres) have been recorded.

Wood Mouse

Apodemus sylvaticus

Size: up to a total length of 20 cm (7¾ in), of which tail is just over half.

Description: large eyes and ears, long tail; yellow-brown above, white below.

Behaviour & breeding: mainly nocturnal. Has elaborate underground runs, but also agile climber. Breeds March to October–December; several litters of up to 9 young, independent at about 3 weeks.

Tracks or signs: hoards of food; feeding platforms, such as old birds' nests, often filled with debris of berries and seeds.

Food: wide variety of seeds, fruits, plant matter and invertebrates.

Yellow-necked mouse (*Apodemus flavicollis*) differs: slightly larger; chest-spots or band.

Yellow-necked mouse.

Wood mice are one of Britain's most widespread and abundant rodents. They are also present throughout most of Europe except northern Scandinavia and north-western USSR. They are found on many islands, and numerous subspecies have been described, including several from Scottish islands where they are often much larger than those on the mainland. Average population densities may vary from 5 per 40 acres (16 hectares), and numbers may fluctuate from year to year. They are important prey for many mammals and birds. Yellow-necked mice have a much more localised distribution in southern England and Wales and are only locally abundant; they are often associated with orchards and apple stores. They also occur west to eastern and southern France and north to Scandinavia and Finland, and sometimes with wood mice in mature woodland

Yellow-necked mouse

Dormouse

Muscardinus avellanarius

> *Size:* total length up to 14 cm (5½ in), of which tail is less than half.
>
> *Description:* bright reddish-brown fur above, white below; long, thickly furred tail.
>
> *Behaviour & breeding:* strictly nocturnal; very arboreal. By day sleeps in nest of grasses and bark or stems. 2 litters a year of 3–4 young which leave the nest at 30 days, independent at 40 days; becomes sexually mature in year following birth.
>
> *Tracks or signs:* nests often in bases of coppiced trees.
>
> *Food:* mainly nuts and seeds; also other vegetable matter.
>
> **Edible dormouse** (*Glis glis*) differs: total length of 30 cm (11¾ in); grey.

Edible dormouse.

Dormice are widespread in Europe, but absent from Iberia and much of Scandinavia. In the British Isles they are mainly confined to southern England and Wales, and absent from Ireland and all islands except the Isle of Wight. They are often associated with hazel coppices, and woodlands with an undergrowth of honeysuckle which they use in their nests. A century ago they were certainly more widespread and more abundant, and were common household pets, achieving fame from the Mad Hatter's tea-party in *Alice in Wonderland*. It is not known if they are continuing to decline. The edible (or fat) dormouse was introduced from continental Europe to a small area north of London in 1902; it has since colonised a small area bordering Beaconsfield, Aylesbury and Luton. It can be confused with the larger grey squirrel.

Dormouse: 1850s
Edible dormouse

Red Fox

Vulpes vulpes

Size: up to 1.2 m (47¼ in) of which tail is a third; up to 40 cm (15¾ in) at shoulder.

Description: reddish-brown; dog-like with pointed muzzle and bushy, usually white-tipped tail.

Behaviour & breeding: variety of loud barks and screams; mainly solitary outside breeding season. Single litter of 3–8 cubs, born in underground earth, usually March–April. Young appear above ground at 24 days, weaned at 8–10 weeks; breed following year.

Tracks or signs: footprints are narrower and more compact than dog's. Earths and paths where foxes cross have distinctive musty odour.

Food: mainly animal matter, including carrion and rodents.

Footprints

The red fox is the most widespread and abundant large predator in Britain, and is found throughout the British Isles including Ireland, but is absent from most islands. In Europe it is ubiquitous, and it was introduced to Australia and New Zealand by British colonists. Foxes occur in almost all habitats including urban centres where they are scavengers. They are considered pests in game-rearing areas and take a significant toll of lambs in hill farms. An average of at least 50 000 foxes are killed in Britain each year by hunting and shooting; this number does not appear to affect the population. In the 1960s severe mortalities were recorded as a result of foxes eating birds and other animals poisoned by pesticide seed dressings; in the late 1970s increased demand for pelts caused an increased. They are one of the main vectors of rabies in continental Europe.

Weasel

Mustela nivalis

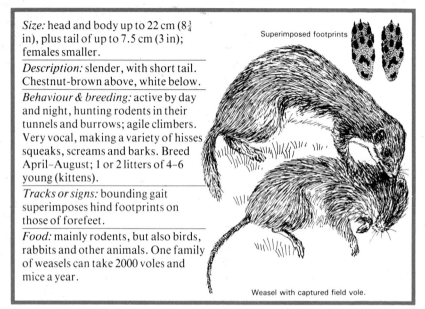

Size: head and body up to 22 cm (8¾ in), plus tail of up to 7.5 cm (3 in); females smaller.

Description: slender, with short tail. Chestnut-brown above, white below.

Behaviour & breeding: active by day and night, hunting rodents in their tunnels and burrows; agile climbers. Very vocal, making a variety of hisses squeaks, screams and barks. Breed April–August; 1 or 2 litters of 4–6 young (kittens).

Tracks or signs: bounding gait superimposes hind footprints on those of forefeet.

Food: mainly rodents, but also birds, rabbits and other animals. One family of weasels can take 2000 voles and mice a year.

Superimposed footprints

Weasel with captured field vole.

The weasel, Britain's smallest carnivore, is found throughout England, Scotland and Wales but is absent from Ireland, the Isle of Man and most smaller islands. It (or a closely related species) is found throughout the temperate northern hemisphere. They are abundant in a wide variety of habitats, particularly woodland, hedgerows and farmland; the populations fluctuate widely, largely depending on the abundance of vole and mice populations, which are their main food. Heavily predated on by man, particularly in areas where pheasants and partridges are reared, they are usually killed with snares or spring-traps. In many parts of the world, they are also trapped extensively for fur which is used as a trimming, but this trade is no longer significant in Britain. Weasels are sometimes taken by owls and other birds of prey.

Stoat

Mustela erminea

Size: head and body up to 30 cm (11¾ in), tail 10 cm (4 in); females smaller.

Description: slender bodied, with short, black-tipped tail. Brown above, creamy-white below; in winter, northern populations may turn completely or partially white, except tail tip.

Behaviour & breeding: active by day and night, often hunting in family groups. Only one litter of up to 12 young (kittens), but normally 5–6. Young are weaned at 5 weeks.

Tracks or signs: tracks similar to weasel, but slightly larger.

Food: mainly rabbits but, since myxomatosis and in areas without rabbits, eats a wide variety of small mammals and other animals.

Stoats are widespread throughout the British Isles, including Ireland, Shetland, the Isle of Man and other islands; they are also found throughout the northern hemisphere. Stoats occur in a wide variety of habitats from lowland woodland and farmlands to open moorlands and mountain and even suburban parks. They are inquisitive animals, and often jump around to attract the attention of birds or rabbits, only to pounce on unsuspecting victims. They have been ruthlessly persecuted by gamekeepers despite the fact that most of their prey is rabbits and rodents; however, where gamekeepering has been reduced or ceased, stoats soon recover in numbers. After the appearance of myxomatosis, stoat numbers dropped drastically. They are extensively trapped for their fur, though not in Britain, the white 'ermine' of the winter pelage being much sought after.

Polecat

Mustela putorius

Size: head and body up to 44 cm (17 in); tail up to 18 cm (7 in).

Description: rather long bodied; dark-brownish with distinctive white pattern on face.

Behaviour & breeding: active by day and night; swims well. Gestation is 42 days; usually 4–5 young (kittens) born April or May, but larger litters recorded. Young weaned at 6–8 weeks.

Tracks or signs: marks territory with strong, foetid secretion, hence alternative name 'foul-mart'.

Food: rodents, young game birds (hence 'poule-chat'), poultry, fish and amphibians.

American mink (*Mustela vison*) differs: usually a uniform dark colour and always lacks the mask.

American mink with duckling prey.

The polecat is widespread over most of western Europe, though densities are often sparce. In Britain it is confined to Wales and adjacent areas. It occurs (or formerly occurred) in a variety of habitats, but is most often in woodlands and hedgerows. It was once common throughout Britain, even in the outskirts of London, and was frequently found living close to human habitation, but by the end of the nineteenth century, persecution by gamekeepers had reduced it to a few isolated populations in central Wales. Since then they have made a considerable recovery. They have been hunted for their pelts and are still important in the fur trade, and were also once hunted with hounds. The American mink escaped from fur farms and was first noted breeding in 1956; since then it has colonised much of the British Isles and in many areas is considered a pest.

Mink

Pine Marten

Martes martes

Size: head and body up to 50 cm (19¾ in); tail up to 27 cm (10¾ in).
Description: slender-bodied. Dark brown with yellow or creamy throat patch; fairly bushy tail.
Behaviour & breeding: active by day and night. Makes dens in rock clefts, old birds' nests, hollow trees, etc. Mates in late summer, but embryo does not develop until following spring. Single litter of up to 5 young (kittens), born in March–April; weaned at 7 weeks.
Tracks or signs: when alarmed, makes 'huffy' noise; other sounds include moans and high-pitched chattering.
Food: mainly rodents and small birds, including voles, squirrels, tits and wrens, as well as beetles and other insects.

The pine marten is found in most of Europe except southern Spain, Portugal and the Balkan peninsula. In the British Isles it is mainly a woodland species, but in some places is found on rocky hillsides. Populations fluctuate according to the availability of food such as squirrels and voles. It was formerly widespread in all suitable habitats, but has been ruthlessly persecuted, both for its valuable pelt and as a predator of gamebirds, despite the fact that it is virtually harmless to sporting interests. With the decline in gamekeepering, it appears to be increasing in some areas, although it is still often killed in snares set for foxes and other animals. Many of the areas from which pine martens have disappeared are now isolated from the remaining populations, thus inhibiting recolonisation, particularly in the eastern and south-western parts of England.

c. 1880

Otter

Lutra lutra

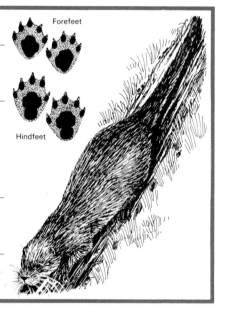

Forefeet

Hindfeet

Size: head and body up to 80 cm (31½ in); tail up to 45 cm (17¾ in).

Description: slender with thick tapering tail. Feet are webbed. Has bounding gait on land, and is an extremely good swimmer.

Behaviour & breeding: usually elusive, solitary and nocturnal, but can be seen by day in undisturbed areas. 2–3 cubs born at almost any time of the year; looked after by female and leave the den at 8 weeks. Young are very playful.

Tracks or signs: footprints in soft mud show webbing; distinctive-smelling 'spraints' deposited on boulders, etc. mark territory.

Food: wide variety of fish, including eels and crayfish, and almost any other animal matter.

The otter extends over most of the Old World in the northern hemisphere; a closely related species is found in North America. It is usually found close to water, both sea and fresh, but travels considerable distances overland. It was formerly hunted with hounds and trapped as vermin; its pelt is still of considerable value in the fur trade. In recent years otters have undergone a catastrophic decline in most of Europe for largely unknown reasons, and have become extinct over a large part of their former range, although it is probable that disturbance, habitat loss and pollution are among the main contributing factors in their decline. In the British Isles they are now extinct or extremely rare over nearly all lowland areas, and the only substantial populations are now in Scotland and Ireland; the population trends in these areas are unknown.

1900s
? Probably present, but declining

Badger

Meles meles

Size: head and body up to 80 cm (31½ in); tail short, less than 20 cm (7¾ in).

Description: robust grey body, short tail and black-and-white face pattern are distinctive.

Behaviour & breeding: lives in small groups in a sett. The 1–5 cubs, born in late winter and spring, come above ground at about 8 weeks and are weaned at 12 weeks; they live together as a family until the autumn or following spring.

Tracks or signs: setts have characteristic mounds of spoil from excavation; scratching on trees, and well-worn paths which go under obstacles.

Food: omnivores; take large numbers of earthworms.

Tuft of hair

The badger is widespread throughout Britain and Ireland, but absent from most islands. They are mainly found in deciduous woodland, but also in farmland and other habitats, particularly when close to pastureland where they can forage for earthworms. Badgers may occur in densities of up to 3 per square mile (2 per sq km), and a single sett may contain up to 12 animals. They were once extensively persecuted, but appear to have increased this century. Now protected, they have been successfully translocated and re-introduced into areas where they had been extirpated. Their only significant predator is man, motor cars taking a substantial toll. In a small area in the south-west, they have been implicated in outbreaks of bovine tuberculosis and have been subjected to an extermination campaign by the Ministry of Agriculture, Fisheries and Food.

■ Occurring relatively dense
▨ Sparse distribution/absent

Wild Cat

Felis silvestris

Size: length to about 1.3 m (51¼ in), of which tail is over one-third.

Description: very similar to domestic cat; tends to be more striped, with black bands on thicker, rather short, blunt tail.

Behaviour & breeding: usually terrestrial. Mates in March, when the male is very noisy; 2–4 kittens born in mid-May. Kittens, reared by female, emerge from den at 5 weeks; weaned at 4 months and independent at 5 months, breeding the following year.

Tracks or signs: footprints virtually indistinguishable from domestic cat's. Droppings large and black, usually deposited near captured prey.

Food: variety of mammals up to size of roe deer kid or lamb; also birds.

Right forefoot

The British wild cat shows some differences from those on the Continent, and has been given the subspecific name *Felis silvestris grampia*. A species of deciduous woodland, it was once widely distributed in western Europe including Britain, but has always been absent from Ireland. In Britain it is now confined to the Scottish Highlands. The last English wild cats disappeared from the Lake District in the mid-nineteenth century, and from Wales at the end of the century. The remnant in Scotland, where they have remained reasonably secure, provided the source for the recolonisation after World War I, and a spread in its range was noticed in 1919. It is now widely distributed in many parts of the Highlands, although virtually nothing is known about population densities. It has been mainly persecuted for its predatory habits, but is protected in Forestry Commission lands.

1880s

Fallow Deer

Cervus dama

Size: adult males up to 1.7 m (67 in) long and 90 cm ($35\frac{1}{2}$ in) at shoulder; females slightly smaller.

Description: typically reddish-brown above with white spots and whitish strip along sides. Antlers are palmate.

Behaviour & breeding: mature males mostly live in bachelor herds. Rut commences in October and lasts about a month. Single fawn born in May or June. Herds re-form in mid-summer.

Tracks or signs: long and slender track; droppings are about 1.5 cm ($\frac{1}{2}$ in) long and black.

Food: graze mainly on grass and herbage, but also browse and sometimes eat bark off trees and raid farm crops.

(a) buck; (b) doe; (c) fawn.

The distribution of the fallow deer has been so altered by man that it is impossible to state with certainty its original distribution—probably the whole of the Mediterranean zone, from Europe to Asia Minor. It now occurs in most parts of Europe except northern Scandinavia, and has been introduced into nearly 40 other countries. It occurs widely (mostly in parks) in southern England, is more scattered in the Midlands and Wales, and is only in a few localities in Scotland. It was introduced in Ireland by the Normans. The favoured habitat is open woodland with clearings where the deer graze, which they do more than other deer. Surprisingly, relatively little is known of their population densities, but densities of 1 per 70 acres (28 hectares) did not do significant damage to Forestry Commission land. The only significant predators, other than man, are foxes which take young fawns.

■ Main distribution
▨ Isolated herds

Red Deer

Cervus elaphus

Sika deer

Size: stags up to 1.2 m (47½ in) at shoulder; hinds smaller.

Description: dark brown, often with greyish tinge; creamy patch on rump. Calves heavily spotted.

Breeding & behaviour: peak of rut is in October, when dominant stag defends harem. Single calf born late May–early June. Weaned at 8–10 months and remain with hind until following autumn.

Tracks or signs: tracks large and rather broad. Droppings 2 cm (¾ in) long; those of males in rut like miniature cow pats.

Food: grasses and heathers, but also browses on tree shoots.

Sika deer (*Cervus nippon*) differs: usually spotted in summer, but uniform in winter.

Britain's largest deer occurs throughout most of Europe, northern Asia and north Africa. In Britain it originally occurred mainly in forests and open woodlands, but its main stronghold is now in the Scottish Highlands, where it moves up to the open moors above the tree-line in summer. Densities of 1 per 15.5 acres (6 hectares) have been maintained in Scotland. They are important game animals, and not only are park herds intensively managed, but so are many wild populations. Present distribution has been considerably affected by man, and indigenous deer are now confined to Exmoor, the Quantocks, the Lake District, the Scottish Highlands and islands, and County Kerry. Sika deer from the Far East were introduced into parks in the nineteenth century and many escapes occurred, particularly between the two world wars. They are now well established.

Roe Deer

Capreolus capreolus

Size: smallest native deer; up to 73 cm (28¾ in) at shoulder.

Description: reddish-brown in summer, rump buff, tail very small; winter coat greyer and thicker. Kids heavily spotted. Antlers short and upright.

Behaviour & breeding: mainly solitary, but form small herds in winter. Rut in late July–August. 2–3 young born following May. Young disperse following spring.

Tracks or signs: footprints up to 4 × 5 cm (1½ × 2 in). Droppings oval, up to 2 cm (¾ in) long, usually black. Trampled rings show where rutting bucks run in circles after does. Bark loudly.

Food: mainly browses on leaves, shoots, but also berries and twigs.

Muntjac

The roe deer occurs mainly in woodland habitats with clearings, and in plantations and more open country. It is absent from most islands, and from Ireland. In Britain, by the late eighteenth century its range was considerably contracted but, during the nineteenth and twentieth centuries, numerous introductions and translocations were made. The Chinese water deer (*Hydropotes inermis*) is an Oriental species which escaped from Woburn Park and Whipsnade; by the 1950s, as a result of further escapes and translocations, it spread rapidly and is now thriving in Bedfordshire, Hampshire, Northamptonshire, Norfolk and Shropshire.

The male has distinctive tusks. Another Oriental, the muntjac (*Muntiacus reevesi*), is well established over most of south-east England. Also known as the 'barking deer', it is secretive and heard more often than seen.

Common Seal

Phoca vitulina

Size: total length: males up to about 1.7 m (67 in), females smaller.

Description: the smallest seal in British waters; darkish grey above, paler below, with numerous dark spots; pups born with adult pelage, occasionally with white coat which is lost almost immediately.

Behaviour & breeding: hauls out on sand banks or rocks. Mating takes place from late July to September. Single pup born June–July, often on temporarily exposed sites from which pup must swim within few hours of birth; young suckle underwater.

Tracks or signs: on sands, flipper marks in pairs with drag of body between.

Food: opportunist; fish, crustaceans, molluscs, etc.

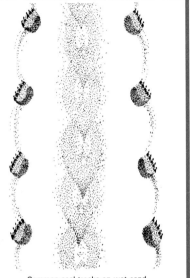

Common seal tracks on wet sand.

The common, or harbour, seal is widely distributed in the northern hemisphere, mainly in coastal waters, but also in estuaries, lochs and, in some areas, freshwater lakes. In Britain the main breeding areas are in East Anglia, Shetland, Orkney, the coasts of Scotland, the Hebrides and Northern Ireland; outside the breeding season, they may occasionally be found in most parts of coastal Britain. They tend to be in small colonies of 30–80 animals, though occasionally in much larger concentrations where food is plentiful. The British Isles population is increasing and currently numbers around 15 000. Hunted locally for pelts and to control depredations on fisheries, most of the hunting is for pups and the total kill in Europe is probably less than 1000. Common seals are protected in England, Scotland and Wales, but may be hunted under licence.

Breeding
Non-breeding

Grey Seal

Halichoerus grypus

Size: total length: males up to 2.3 m
(90½ in); females to 1.95 m (76¾ in).

Description: rather variable colour;
bulls generally darker than cows.
White at birth, moulting into adult
pelage at about 10 days old.

Behaviour & breeding: hauls out on
traditional sites, which usually differ
from breeding sites. Breeding season
varies regionally; pups born mainly
September–January; mating season is
during same period in most colonies,
when bulls are strongly territorial.
Very vocal; wide variety of noises.

Tracks or signs: on sand, flipper
marks in pairs with drag of body
between.

Food: very varied; fish, molluscs,
crustaceans, etc. Occasionally
damage fish in nets.

Grey seal cow with suckling pup.

The grey seal is widespread in the North Atlantic
and adjacent waters, with the largest concen-
tration occurring in British waters. Since the
beginning of this century the number of grey
seals in these waters has increased dramatically,
particularly in the last 30 years, the increase
estimated to be approximately 9 per cent per
annum. The grey seal has been the focus of
considerable controversy concerning the
damage it causes to fisheries. In the late
1970s the UK Government decided
on a policy designed to reduce
the population, but opposition
from various conservation
bodies resulted in a complete
review of policy in relation to
grey seals and fisheries
management. Recent offshore
oil drilling in Scottish waters
poses a potential threat to grey seal
colonies. It is protected in England, Scotland
and Wales but can be hunted under licence.

Breeding
Non-breeding

Killer Whale

Orca orcinus

Size: males up to 9 m (30 ft); females smaller.

Description: largest member of dolphin family. Basically black, with white on underside, a pale patch on flanks and a white patch on side of head (in young, patches may be tan). Dorsal fin large (up to 1.8 m, 6 ft), erect and triangular.

Behaviour: travel in groups of up to 25 or 30, occasionally many more. Fast swimmers (up to 25 knots). Often seen with head and forequarters exposed.

Tracks or signs: 'pitchpoles' (hanging vertically in water with head clear); also 'porpoises'.

Food: squid, fish (especially salmon), seabirds, seals, other whales and dolphins.

Killer whale 'pitchpoling'.

The killer whale is found in all oceans surrounding the British Isles. They are most frequently recorded off the west coast and off Scotland, particularly where deep waters approach the shore, and have only rarely been recorded from the south and east coasts. Most of the sightings in northern Britain have been in June and, further south, later in the summer; they are rarely seen in winter months. The movements of killer whales are probably linked with those of their food supply. In order to kill large whales, they gather in large packs. They have been hunted by the whaling industry and a few have been captured for performing in dolphinaria, but little is known about their population trends. The false killer whale (*Pseudorca crassideus*) is smaller than the killer, growing to about 5.5 m (18 ft), and all black. There have been occasional mass strandings.

Sperm Whale

Physeter catodon

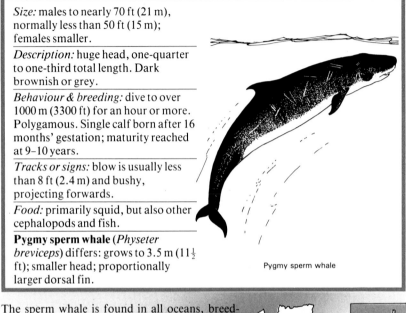

Size: males to nearly 70 ft (21 m), normally less than 50 ft (15 m); females smaller.

Description: huge head, one-quarter to one-third total length. Dark brownish or grey.

Behaviour & breeding: dive to over 1000 m (3300 ft) for an hour or more. Polygamous. Single calf born after 16 months' gestation; maturity reached at 9–10 years.

Tracks or signs: blow is usually less than 8 ft (2.4 m) and bushy, projecting forwards.

Food: primarily squid, but also other cephalopods and fish.

Pygmy sperm whale (*Physeter breviceps*) differs: grows to 3.5 m (11½ ft); smaller head; proportionally larger dorsal fin.

Pygmy sperm whale

The sperm whale is found in all oceans, breeding in warm tropical waters and migrating to cooler waters during the summer months. The males migrate to polar regions and all the sperm whales recorded off Britain have been males. Sperm whales are hunted for spermaceti and other oils, and their worldwide population has been considerably reduced through over-hunting; even their average size has declined. In the days of 'Moby Dick' 90-ft (27 m) animals were recorded, and even in the 1890s 70-ft (21 m) specimens were recorded. In the 1930s most males killed were around 55 ft (16.5 m) long, but by 1972 most were around 48 ft (14.5 m). For over 100 years there have been strong selective pressures on the large bulls. The pygmy sperm whale has been stranded in Ireland. Very little is known about its range, and it is rarely seen at sea.

Fin Whale

Balaenoptera physalus

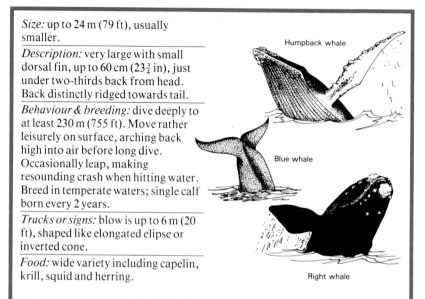

Size: up to 24 m (79 ft), usually smaller.

Description: very large with small dorsal fin, up to 60 cm (23¾ in), just under two-thirds back from head. Back distinctly ridged towards tail.

Behaviour & breeding: dive deeply to at least 230 m (755 ft). Move rather leisurely on surface, arching back high into air before long dive. Occasionally leap, making resounding crash when hitting water. Breed in temperate waters; single calf born every 2 years.

Tracks or signs: blow is up to 6 m (20 ft), shaped like elongated elipse or inverted cone.

Food: wide variety including capelin, krill, squid and herring.

Humpback whale

Blue whale

Right whale

Widely distributed in all oceans, though considerably reduced in numbers, the fin whale, or common rorqual, has been hunted commercially since *c.*1900 and, although severely depleted, small numbers are still taken. Commercial fisheries formerly operated from Ireland and Scotland, taking fin whales as they migrated northwards. In the first three decades of this century 4356 were killed off Shetland, 1492 off the Outer Hebrides and 592 off Ireland. The north Atlantic population is still hunted by Icelandic whalers. The blue whale (*B. musculus*) also occurs in British waters. The largest known mammal, growing to a length of over 30 m (100 ft), it too has been extensively hunted and its population worldwide has been estimated as low as 2500. The humpback whale and the nearly extinct right whale also occur around Britain, particularly the west.

More abundant

Minke Whale

Balaenoptera acutorostrata

Size: up to 9 m (30 ft).

Description: smallest baleen whale in the Atlantic. Black to dark grey above, white beneath. Tall fin about two-thirds back. Distinctive white patch on flippers. Baleen mostly yellowish-white at front, brownish at back.

Behaviour & breeding: usually found singly or in groups of 2 or 3; may gather around concentrations of food. Often approach boats closely, particularly stationary or drifting boats. Single calf is born in winter.

Tracks or signs: blow is low and inconspicuous.

Food: mainly small fish, particularly capelin; also krill and squid.

Sei whale (*B. borealis*) differs: grows to over 18 m (60 ft).

The minke whale (also called the little piked whale or lesser rorqual) is found in all oceans and is now the commonest rorqual around the British Isles, particularly in the west. The single calf, born each year after a gestation of 10 months, becomes sexually mature at 6–8 years. It has been suggested that, particularly in the Antarctic but also in northern waters, minke whales have been able to increase in numbers because of the depletion to near extinction of several of the larger species of whales. It probably migrates to the North Sea and the Norwegian coast via the north of Scotland. The sei whale (*B. borealis*) also occurs in British waters, most often in June off the west coast of Britain. Once schools numbered hundreds, but now they are not particularly abundant. They usually rise to the surface at a shallow angle, with the back exposed at the same time.

Possible occurrence

Pilot Whale

Globiocephala melaena

Size: males up to 6 m (20 ft); females smaller.

Description: rather long and slender with bulbous head, low fin and long, pointed flippers (up to one-fifth of body length). All black except white throat and underside.

Behaviour & breeding: gregarious, in schools of about 20. Calves born every 3–4 years, after gestation of 16 months; weaned at 22 months, sexually mature at 6–7 years (females), 12 years (males). Young are over 1.5 m (5 ft) at birth.

Tracks or signs: at a distance the most distinctive feature is dorsal fin set well forward.

Food: mainly cuttlefish.

Risso's dolphin

The pilot whale, also known as the caa'ing whale, pothead or blackfish, is fairly common around Britain and Ireland, and is also widely distributed in the rest of the north Atlantic. It probably occurs in all months of the year, but is most abundant from April to October. It has been hunted from earliest times, whole schools being driven ashore and butchered. This form of hunting persists in the Faeroes, but no longer in the British Isles. Unlike most other cetaceans, the pilot whale may have increased in numbers around the British Isles; since 1913 (when detailed records were first started) the numbers of strandings has shown a steady increase. This may possibly be associated with the reduction in hunting. Risso's dolphin (*Grampus griseus*) is rather similar, but smaller; it is common around most of the British Isles, and seen in most months.

More abundant

Common Porpoise

Phocoena phocoena

Size: about 1.5 m (5 ft).

Description: smallest British cetacean; short blunt head, no 'beak'. Dark brown or blackish above, fading to greyish white on sides, and white below. Triangular fin.

Behaviour & breeding: occurs in schools which may number 100 or more, but usually smaller. Swims slowly, rarely leaping clear of water. Single calf born in summer after gestation of 11 months; sexual maturity reached at 3–4 years.

Tracks or signs: often swim on surface with distinctive 'porpoising' action. One of most frequently seen cetaceans.

Food: mainly fish, crustaceans and cuttlefish.

The common, or harbour, porpoise is widely distributed in the coastal waters of the north Atlantic, and is the most commonly seen cetacean around the British Isles, and also one of the most frequently stranded. It occurs mainly in harbours, bays, estuaries and other shallow waters, and is usually seen in small groups of up to 10 individuals. They do not ride bow waves and are rather shy, and are easily disturbed by engine noise from boats. Although adults with calves are found in coastal waters on both sides of the Atlantic from July to October, the precise breeding site is unknown. They have been hunted commercially in many parts of the world, and there were formerly fisheries in the Baltic and off the Dutch coast. They do not normally associate with dolphins, but are sometimes seen with the larger whales.

Most abundant

Common Dolphin

Delphinus delphis

Size: up to about 2.5 m (8 ft); males slightly larger than females.

Description: rather slender, with a beak; medium-size fin. Dark above, white below, with elaborate pattern of light and dark bands and yellow on sides.

Behaviour & breeding: usually in schools of over 1000, sometimes mixed with other species. Often approach boats from considerable distances. Breeding is little known; gestation 10 months, with young born mainly in summer and autumn.

Tracks or signs: frequently rides bow waves and jumps clear of water.

Food: wide variety of fish and cephalopods.

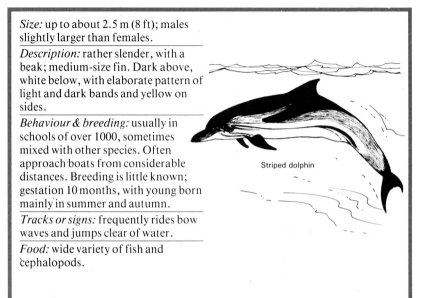

Striped dolphin

The fast-swimming common, or saddleback, dolphin is found in all temperate and tropical oceans, and is relatively abundant around the British Isles, but less frequent in Scottish waters and rarely in the North Sea. The numbers of strandings of common dolphins have steadily declined since the beginning of this century, suggesting a decline in population. This decline and also changes in their distribution are closely connected with changes in their food supply. Most sightings of common dolphin are from June to September when the school sizes are also larger, sometimes numbering 1000 or more. Common dolphins are extremely similar to striped, or Euphrosyne, dolphins (*Stenella caeruleoalbus*), but these have only rarely been recorded from British waters; they are the most common species in the Mediterranean, and have thin black lines running from their eyes to the flippers and down the sides.

Bottle-nosed Dolphin

Tursiops truncatus

Size: up to 3.7 m (12 ft).

Description: fairly large dolphin weighing up to 650 kg (1430 lb). Dark grey above, white below (sometimes with pinkish flush); distinct 'beak', and prominent fin.

Behaviour & breeding: usually in small schools of up to 10 animals, but can be in much larger groups. Often associates with other dolphins and whales. Single young born in summer after gestation of about 12 months; sexual maturity reached at about 12 years.

Tracks or signs: frequently ride bow waves and surf, and jump clear of water.

Food: fish, crustaceans, cephalopods, etc. Often feeds on fish stirred up by boats.

White-sided dolphin (top) and white-beaked dolphin

The bottle-nosed dolphin is the species most commonly seen in dolphinaria. In the wild it is widely distributed in the north Atlantic and Mediterranean, and (after porpoises) is one of the most common cetaceans around the British Isles; it is most abundant in the south and west. During the breeding season, schools contain both sexes, but at other times they are segregated. These dolphins are very active and in captivity learn to perform many tricks. The wild ones help young and wounded dolphins and have been known to help drowning humans to the surface. The white-sided dolphin (*Lagenorhynchus acutus*) and the white-beaked dolphin (*L. albirostris*) also occur commonly in British waters, the white-sided particularly in the North Sea. Both species have rather northerly distributions in British waters, and congregate primarily in small schools.

Conclusions and the Future

The mammal fauna of Britain was changing and evolving long before humans (also mammals) arrived on the scene, and there is evidence to suggest that changes in distribution and density of many species will continue.

Some species, such as the otter and red squirrel, will almost certainly become locally extinct, at least in England, and will only survive in Scotland. Several bats will also probably join the mouse-eared bat by becoming extinct. Perhaps surprisingly, with increased urbanisation, and even suburbanisation, the mole, too, is likely to disappear from large areas—particularly in the south-east. It is not tolerated even in suburban areas where it spoils tennis courts, golf courses, football pitches and private lawns. As suburbanisation spreads, so the mole is pushed into isolated pockets, and eventually disappears when these pockets are no longer of sufficient size to maintain variable populations.

The Ministry of Agriculture, Fisheries and Food has indicated its intention to eradicate the coypu in East Anglia, and already it has had its range considerably reduced and is now being held in check by trapping. The intention is to eliminate it with a massive campaign after a severe winter. However, the nature of the habitat where a number of the remnant populations survive makes it rather unlikely that it will be possible to totally exterminate them.

On the other hand, comparatively newly arrived introductions, such as American mink, are clearly here to stay, and unless the nature of land management reverts to that of the nineteenth century and intensive gamekeepering recommences, they are likely to continue to increase. The same is true of the polecat and pine marten—their spread may well even start to accelerate soon. The spread of the wild cat may well continue—although what will happen when it comes into greater contact with domestic cats is not known. The Chinese water deer already has a firm foothold in East Anglia and it is quite likely to become firmly established and increase in this area, and the muntjac has been steadily spreading through the woodlands of southern England.

Just as in the last few decades a number of alien species have

Coypu (right) and water vole.

managed to become established in the mammal fauna of the British Isles, before the end of the century a few more will almost certainly have become established, either as a result of deliberate introductions or of escapes.

Proposals have already been made for re-introducing beavers into Britain but, although they have received a degree of support, they are unlikely to go ahead. This is perhaps unfortunate since there is a wealth of experience which can be drawn upon from similar experiments in France and Switzerland. Also, the beaver is a sufficiently large and slow-breeding animal so that, should the experiment be a failure, it would be possible to eliminate them relatively easily.

Among accidental introductions, it is impossible to predict new colonists; with modern air travel and even fast sea travel, bats, rats and mice are all possibilities. Under the Rabies Act, the import of exotic mammals is difficult and, because of quarantine, expensive.

Consequently, the wide variety of exotic mammals which were formerly available from pet dealers has largely gone. However, captive-bred chipmunks, raccoons, racoon-like dogs and Arctic foxes are only a few of the species which are available relatively cheaply from dealers. Gerbils and hamsters have already bred in the wild and it could be predicted that one day both species, possibly together with cavies, could become established. Finally, porcupines have escaped from wildlife parks and live and breed in the wild, and they could easily become established as serious pests.

It is the normal policy of most government departments concerned with the possible introduction of exotic wildlife, as well as that of the voluntary bodies, to oppose attempts to introduce further species. However, there are some arguments in favour of introducing exotic species. First, there is very little of Britain that can be described in any way as natural—virtually the whole landscape has been altered or modified by man at some time or other. Second, some species have specialised requirements and, because of their behaviour or other factors, could be closely managed, as with the red-necked wallabies of the Peak District. However, the introduction of species known to be potential pests—such as the North American cottontail rabbit, the European hamster or Himalayan porcupine—is obviously undesirable.

If present trends continue, it is likely that Britain's bat populations will be very much reduced for many years to come. Bats have been affected by a wide variety of environmental factors but, more importantly, the meagre covering of woodland in Britain probably means that several species which have small populations will become extinct if additional pressures threaten them. The extensive use of persistant pesticides in the 1960s undoubtedly had a deleterious effect on many bat populations and, being long-lived, slow-reproducing species, they will take many years to recuperate. In addition, the depleted populations have suffered further from a series of poor summers when, because of bad weather at crucial times of the year, whole colonies failed to rear any young, thus eliminating a complete generation. On top of all this, bat habitats in the form of mature woodland and marshes are disappearing at an alarming rate, while roosting sites such as hollow trees are being destroyed, and old mines and even cellars as well as caves are subject to increasing amounts of disturbance—yet more factors contributing to their decline. Unless strict protection and active conservation measures are promoted, the outlook for Britain's bats is not very bright.

By contrast, our seals are thriving. The grey seal population has had a veritable explosion and, although not too healthy in the south and west, in Scotland and the northern isles it is flourishing. In recent years the Department of Agriculture and Fisheries for Scotland has tried to introduce seal hunts, ostensibly to reduce pressure from seals on fish stocks although, as yet, it has not been demonstrated that grey seals have a significant effect on these stocks. Consequently, as a result of public pressure, the Government has postponed further seal hunts pending the collecting of further data on the effects of seals on fisheries. In the future it can be predicted that the populations will continue to grow, but will no doubt stabilise unless they expand to recolonise some of the places where they once bred, such as the coasts of northern Europe from France to Denmark.

Under protection, there is evidence that some of the great whale populations are gradually, albeit slowly, recovering. In the Outer Hebrides, off Ireland and the Shetlands, on the routes of the migrating whales where there were once whaling stations, it is quite likely that boatloads of tourists will be going whale-watching—just like they do in the St Lawrence in Canada or off Cape Cod in the USA.

Glossary

baleen: horny fibres in the upper jaws of the great whales (except sperm whales), used for straining food from the sea.

blow: commonly known as the 'spout'; the column of water droplets produced by whales when surfacing to breathe.

bow waves: waves produced by a boat at its pointed end; often ridden by dolphins and porpoises.

buck: male roe deer, fallow deer or muntjac.

bull: male whale or cattle.

calf: young whale, porpoise, cattle or red deer.

cow: female whale or cattle.

capelin: fish important in the diet of whales, particularly minke whales.

carnivore: predatory, flesh-eating animal.

cavernicolous: inhabitant of caves.

cephalopod: marine moluscs with tentacles, e.g., squid, octopus, cuttlefish.

cetaceans: marine mammals including whales, dolphins and porpoises.

cub: young badger, fox or otter.

diurnal: day-living; opposite of nocturnal.

doe: female fallow deer, roe deer or muntjac.

drey: nest of squirrel.

earth: burrow of fox.

fawn: young fallow deer, muntjac or Chinese water deer.

feral: when a domestic animal has reverted to the wild.

form: lair of hare.

fraying: abrasion of trees and bushes caused by deer rubbing their antlers to clean off the velvet covering them.

hibernacula: places of hibernation.

hind: female red deer or sika deer.

kid: young roe deer.

kitten: young stoat, weasel, polecat, pine marten or wild cat.

krill: small planktonic animals forming the main prey of the great whales; particularly Euphasians (shrimp-like creatures).

leveret: young hare; also used locally for young rabbits.

mandibles: jaws.

montane: of mountains.

myxomatosis: viral, flea-borne disease of rabbits, originally from South America.

nose-leaf: elaborate structure of Rhinolophid bats (e.g., horseshoe bats), used in sound production for echo-location.

omnivore: animal which eats both plant and animal matter.

pelage: fur.

pitchpoling: of whales and dolphins: 'standing' in water with the front half of the body above the surface, using tail flukes to 'tread' water.

predation: feeding on other animals.

pup: young common seal or grey seal.

rut: mating period of deer.

sett (set): burrows of badgers.

slots: footprints of deer.

spermaceti: waxy substance from head of sperm whale, used for candles and ointments.

spraints: droppings of otter.

stag: male red deer or fallow deer.

tump: mole-hill.

vector: carrier of diseases or parasites (e.g., black rats as carriers of the plague or red foxes as vectors of rabies).

velvet: soft covering of newly grown deer antlers.